CORNWALL
STRANGE BUT TRUE

JOAN RENDELL

The History Press

First published in 2007 by Sutton Publishing Limited

Reprinted in 2009 by
The History Press
The Mill, Brimscombe Port,
Stroud, Gloucestershire, GL5 2QG
www.thehistorypress.co.uk

British Library Cataloguing in Publication Data
A catalogue record for this book is available from the British Library.

ISBN 978-0-7509-4623-0

Typeset in 10.5/13.5pt Janson.
Typesetting and origination by
Sutton Publishing Limited.
Printed and bound in Great Britain by
Marston Book Services Limited, Oxford

CONTENTS

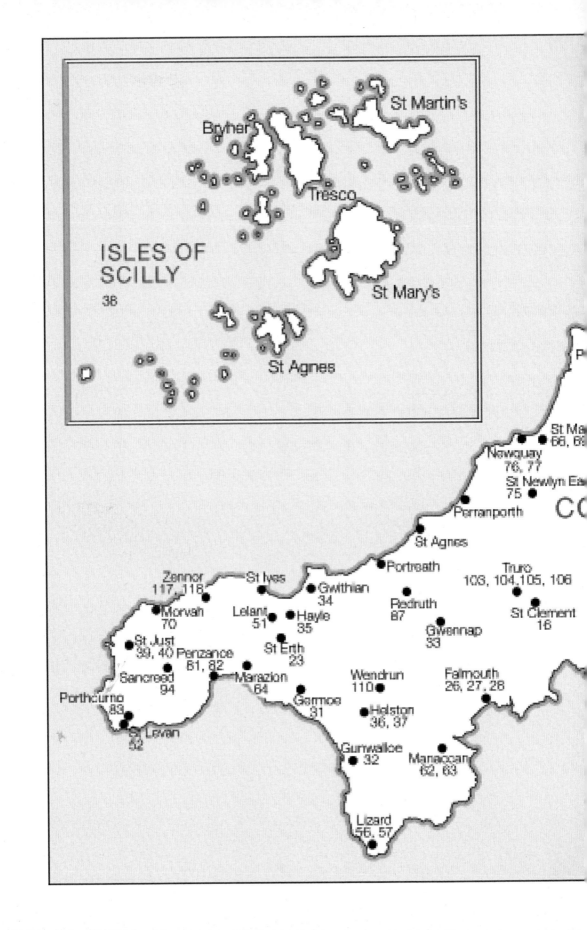

ISLES OF
SCILLY
36

St Martin's

Bryher

Tresco

St Mary's

St Agnes

P

St Ma
66, 69

Newquay
76, 77

St Newlyn Ea
75

CO

Perranporth

St Agnes

Portreath

Truro
103, 104, 105, 106

Zennor
117, 118

St Ives

Gwithian
34

Redruth
87

St Clement
16

Morvah
70

Lelant
51

Hayle
35

Gwennap
33

St Just
39, 40

Penzance
81, 82

St Erth
23

Sancreed
94

Marazion
64

Wendrun
110

Falmouth
26, 27, 28

Porthcurno
83

Gurlnoe
31

Helston
36, 37

St Levan
52

Gunwalloe
32

Manaccan
62, 63

Lizard
56, 57

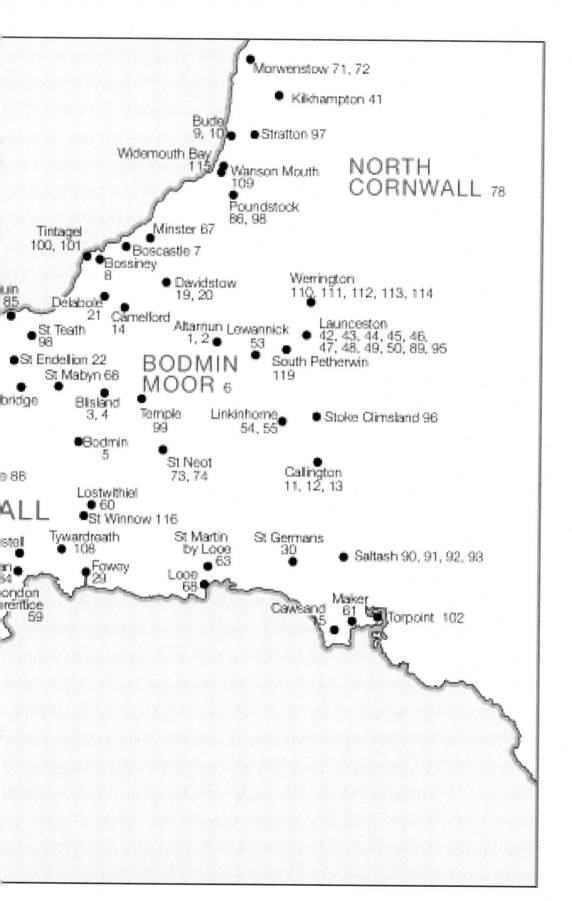

Morwenstow 71, 72

Kilkhampton 41

Bude
9, 10   Stratton 97

Widemouth Bay
115   Wanson Mouth
109

NORTH
CORNWALL 78

Poundstock
86, 98

Tintagel
100, 101   Minster 67   Werrington
110, 111, 112, 113, 114
Boscastle 7
Bossiney
8

Davidstow
19, 20

uin
85   Delabole
21   Camelford
14   Altarnun
1, 2   Lewannick
53   Launceston
42, 43, 44, 45, 46,
47, 48, 49, 50, 89, 95

St Teath
98

St Endellion 22
St Mabyn 68

BODMIN
MOOR 6

South Petherwin
119

bridge   Blisland
3, 4   Temple
99   Linkinhorne
54, 55   Stoke Climsland 96

Bodmin
5

St Neot
73, 74   Callington
11, 12, 13

e 86

Lostwithiel
60
St Winnow 116

ALL   Tywardreath
108   St Martin
by Looe
63   St Germans
30   Saltash 90, 91, 92, 93

stell

Fowey
29   Looe
68

rn
4
ondon
srentice
59   Cawsand
5   Maker
61   Torpoint 102

FOREWORD

I have known Joan Rendell both as a friend and professionally for almost twenty years, during which time I have listened to numerous anecdotes and read many of her previous twenty-eight books which have never failed to amaze me. Joan has been a trusted and reliable contributor to the *Cornish & Devon Post* series for over sixty years and latterly a whole series of interesting articles on the parishes of Bodmin Moor written by her have been published in the comparatively recently launched *North Cornwall Post & Diary*. I deem it a great honour to pen these few words to a lady who, through her fantastic use of words and her extensive knowledge of so many subjects, guarantees 'a good read' to all who pick up any of her books and this one – her twenty-ninth – is certainly no exception . . . enjoy it dear reader.

Geoff Seccombe
General Manager, Editor and Director
Cornish & Devon Post series and associated titles

INTRODUCTION

C ornwall is different – its people, its dialect, its general atmosphere is unique. It may have something to do with the fact that Cornwall is the county with the most coastline in Britain and even has a popular beach generated by one of its own industries. Strange but true – you can't get much more different than that. This book hopes to reveal some of the curiosities of Cornwall which are unknown outside the county and even to a lot of people living there today.

It is little wonder that Cornwall has many interesting features; some man-made, some natural and many unique to the 'toe' of England which can boast lots of 'firsts' – the first wireless communication, originated in Cornwall by Marconi; his first telegraph communication cable to reach across the Atlantic from a Cornish beach, and so on. For hundreds, even thousands of years Cornwall was a highly industrialised area. Tin mining was carried out from time immemorial; the discovery of china clay led to Cornwall providing one-quarter of the world's output of that very useful commodity, and for a county almost surrounded by sea, fishing has always been a major industry.

In the Bronze Age Bodmin Moor had quite vast prehistoric settlements with clusters of dwellings, the inhabitants of which found plenty to occupy their time. And those early people left their mark in a remarkable way with their enormous standing stones and burial chambers. The mystic atmosphere of those very early days still remains and there are many who believe that the massive stones erected by their ancestors are still 'alive'. If one is 'tuned in' (as a surprising number of Cornish people are), placing the palm of the hand against a standing stone (the higher up the better) will produce a sensation like a mild electric shock. However, if any such stones have been moved or re-erected after they have fallen they are 'dead' and no sensations are felt.

The Cornish language died out in the early nineteenth century, but is now being revived by several groups of enthusiasts who would like it to rank alongside Welsh as a living language with bilingual speakers.

Cornish mining skills were employed all over the world, and as the old saying goes: wherever in the world you saw a big pit there was a Cousin Jack (a Cornishman) at the bottom of it. The mines, pilchard industry, china clay and granite quarrying were all major industries in Cornwall and employed thousands of men and women.

Now all the mines have closed, the pilchard industry is dead since the 'little silver darlings' deserted the seas around Cornwall, the china clay industry is in decline owing to foreign competition and agriculture does not employ as many as it used to. To some extent tourism has taken the place of these traditional industries, but it can never take the place of the old Cornwall of which every Cornishman and woman is so proud.

To be Cornish is something special; to share in its mysticism and history is a privilege and the county still holds many puzzles which even in this modern age have never been solved. One of them is included in this book. Do you have any theories?

Joan Rendell

ACKNOWLEDGEMENTS

I am deeply indebted to the following for the use of photographs and information (not in alphabetical order but as they were received): Joyce Greenham, W. Mills, Christine Parnell, Colin Squire and Saltash Heritage Centre, Beryl Tapp, John Neale, Robert Evans, David and Carol Stark, Harry Woodhouse, P. King, David Clarke, L.E. Pierce, the Revd A. Rowell, Rosemary Pritchard and Newquay Old Cornwall Society, 'Bill' Glanville, Michael Tangye, MBE, Andrew Langdon, Brian Pritchard, Terry Knight, Steve Hartgroves and the Historic Environment Service Cornwall County Council, Stuart B. Smith OBE, Bob Acton, Howard Phillips (Howard Phillips Photography), Gerald Fry, John Lyne, the late Sir Alan Dalton and Westgate Studios. Without their help it would not have been possible to record and show some of the very unusual things which are to be seen in our lovely county of Cornwall.

STRANGE BUT TRUE

ALTARNUN

Corn Dollies

1

Altarnun church, known as the Cathedral of the Moor, has a splendid array of sixteenth-century bench ends carved by a local craftsman who trawled every aspect of parish life in pursuit of his subjects and succeeded in depicting something which, as far as is known, does not feature on any other bench end anywhere in Britain.

It shows a corn dolly; not the sort that is seen in craft shops today but the sixteenth-century version of the fertility symbol that celebrated the harvest. In those days a corn dolly was a crude effigy of a human figure that was carried around the church. The figure is thought to have been based on Isis, wife and sister of Osiris, the corn god of Egyptian mythology, who was said to have discovered barley and wheat growing wild. She persuaded Osiris to grow it for the benefit of his people, who made him their corn god.

Two poles were lashed together in the form of a cross and the upright pole pushed through the centre of a sheaf of wheat. Bundles of wheat were then tied to the arms of the cross and the sheaf fastened tightly at the top to form a head and around the middle to form a waist. The carving clearly shows the stalks of corn in the form of a 'skirt'. It was a pagan custom brought into the church, combining the two beliefs, which was in no way considered inappropriate at the time.

ALTARNUN

Goose Holes

2

Bodmin Moor hides many gems and none more precious than Codda, a Grade II* listed farmstead in the parish of Altarnun. The buildings were originally one of four farmsteads within a medieval hamlet. Its inhabitants would have worked the ancient strip fields which still exist beyond the margins of the nineteenth-century field system. The people would have ploughed, tilled and cultivated the land with the most primitive tools, as well as tending their stock.

Codda retains medieval features unique to the area, one of which is its row of goose holes. These little stone caverns were constructed for the purpose of penning geese at night to keep them safe from predators such as foxes; they also provided a dry and comparatively warm environment for the birds in the harsh winter weather. There is a more 'modern' curiosity attached to the holding. The Victorian privy constructed above a stream (no elaborate plumbing needed!) is a cosy two-seater where husband and wife could sit side by side.

BLISLAND

3

The 'Living' Picture

Blisland is a pretty village with a Norman church, much restored in Victorian times and dedicated to Saints Protus and Hyacinth who,

despite their feminine-sounding names, were both men who lived in the third century.

In the church is a real curiosity: a framed reproduction of a painting of Jesus Christ by Gabriel Max, an Austrian artist born in 1840. The original is in a collection in Prague and is valued at a high five-figure sum. The extraordinary thing about the painting is that it is an optical illusion; if the eyes are watched closely they will suddenly open. In the reproduction and even in photographs of it this most surprising and clever illusion is still 100 per cent effective. An inscription on the reproduction tells us that fourteen colours were used in the painting to get the strange effect. The inscription also says that the painting is known as 'St Veronica's Handkerchief' but that is a total misnomer.

4

4

BLISLAND

Jubilee Rock

There are plenty of giant boulders on Bodmin Moor but none like Jubilee Rock on Pendrift Common, near Blisland. It is 700ft above sea level and an unlikely commemoration in an even more unlikely setting.

In 1809 a Lieutenant Rogers, son of a local resident, had an idea to commemorate the Golden Jubilee of King George III by carving on the rock on the Common where he had played as a child. It was a strange notion. Lieutenant Rogers carved into the hard granite the Royal Arms, coats of arms (some of local families), symbols of agriculture, industry, commerce and plenty, and other emblems which took his fancy, including a figure of Britannia. Lieutenant Rogers also composed a patriotic poem to accompany the carving and had the verses engraved on a brass plate which was fixed to the boulder, but it was removed over 100 years ago, for what reason is not known. Carvings of Queen Victoria's name and monogram were added to the stone in later years. It has become a unique monument. Seeing it in such a remote place is a quite bizarre experience the first time one comes upon it.

5

BODMIN
A Royal Dog's Memorial

Until comparatively recent times Cornwall had some royal residents. Prince Chula Chakrabongse and his cousin Prince Bira of Siam (now Thailand) lived for many years at the country house called Tredethy (now a hotel) near Bodmin. Prince Bira was a famous Grand Prix motor-racing driver both before and after the Second World War. Prince Chula

and his English wife (the former Miss Elizabeth Hunter) took a great interest in local life and activities; they were generous benefactors to Bodmin and gave the Narissa Hall in Priory Park to the town to mark their infant daughter's first birthday. It is named after her.

Both Prince Chula and Prince Bira served in the Home Guard during the war and Princess Chula became superintendent of the St John Ambulance Brigade, giving valuable voluntary service in that capacity.

Prince and Princess Chula came to Cornwall in 1938 and lived at Rock before moving into Tredethy. Their daughter was born in 1956. Sadly Prince Chula died in 1963 at the age of only 55 and his wife died eight years later on her 56th birthday.

Prince Chula was a great animal lover and a permanent tribute to his compassion and devotion is in the Priory car park. It takes the form of a granite memorial incorporating a drinking bowl for dogs, and bears the inscription 'Presented by His Royal Highness Prince Chula of Siam in memory of his friend JOAN, a wire haired terrier who died in 1948 in her 17th year. Further endowed in memory of the bulldog HERCULES 1954'. The drinking bowl is always kept full of clean water and is much appreciated by both the canine population of Bodmin after their runs in Priory Park and by visitors' pets who stop in the car park.

BODMIN MOOR

6

Amethyst

Amethyst is prized as a semi-precious stone, the largest provider of it being Brazil, but what is not always known is that samples could come from much nearer home, because there is a rich vein of amethyst running across Bodmin Moor.

This violet variety of crystalline quartz was believed by the ancient Greeks to be a remedy for drunkenness, while other ancient civilisations regarded it as a preventive of intoxication.

The darkest and finest vein of amethyst used to be seen in the china clay workings at Hawks Tor Pit on Bodmin Moor. When the pit was operational, as the monitors moved around the pit, washing out the clay with their extremely powerful jets of water, the amethyst was exposed. It was over 1ft wide and a beautiful sight, the purple shining in the sunlight against the white of the clay. As the monitors moved around in their endless circumnavigation of the pit the seam remained exposed. I was once given permission to enter the pit to witness this marvel of nature and was actually able to collect a number of samples of the stone as it lay on the surface. In fact, my own platinum engagement ring features a Bodmin Moor amethyst set between small diamonds. As the seam continues east the amethyst becomes paler in colour; it surfaces again at Parsons Park Pit, near Bolventor. Here it is often possible to pick up small samples of the paler amethyst in chippings by the side of the road, the granite chippings having been used as road surface materials for the road into the pit.

Unfortunately, it is no longer possible to see the Hawks Tor Pit seam. The pit was taken out of use and closed several years ago; it was allowed to flood and is now a big lake and the distinctive china clay waste 'mountain' beside the pit, which was a well-known landmark from the A30, has been levelled. But the amethyst is still there and if the pit is ever reopened it will once more become visible.

7

BOSCASTLE

Forrabury Stitches

This agricultural oddity is the best preserved open field system in Cornwall; indeed, the stitchmeal system or stitchfield cultivation plots, once widespread, now survives in only a handful of places in Britain and the one in Boscastle is a classic example. The area, sometimes described as a common, extends to some 80 acres, and medieval and seventeenth-century sherds have been found in the area.

The stitches is one of only two walled agricultural terraces in southern Britain and therefore has an important place in the history of British agriculture. Nowadays, there are only about forty strips surviving from an original total of over sixty, and there was a fear at one time that the stitches would disappear altogether. Fortunately, they were saved by the National Trust, so their future is assured.

An essential part of the management is that each strip is cultivated at least once every four years, the crops being oats, corn and grass, the latter being cut as winter feed for stock. Stubble on the arable stitches is left as cover and a food source for overwintering birds such as finches and buntings. This type of management provides a unique habitat for plants;

some which grow there are very rare in other parts of Britain. The area is designated as a Site of Special Scientific Interest.

Two permissive paths have been created in order to overcome some of the conflicts of use by walkers; owners of dogs are asked to keep them on leads while using these paths and to avoid walking across the middle of the stitches.

Incidentally, the word 'stitch' has no dictionary meaning in connection with agriculture so one assumes that the Forrabury layout of fields is unique in more ways than one.

BOSSINEY

The Petrifying Well

8

It does not get any publicity and most people do not even know that it exists, but the petrifying well at Bossiney has the same powers as the famous petrifying well at Knaresborough in Yorkshire, which is known and visited by thousands of people.

The well at Bossiney is situated in a deep valley which runs down to the sea and access is not easy as it involves scrambling down a very steep

grassy slope. Debris such as empty snail shells, even living plants such as liverwort, get turned into stone by the action of the water constantly washing over them. As the water forces them down they congeal into lumps of petrified material, the components of which are clearly recognisable.

As far as is known, Bossiney is Cornwall's only petrifying well. It is not spectacular, just a little stream meandering along with a slightly deeper pool in which the debris gathers – a hidden gem.

BUDE

9

The Bude Light

It is a modern curiosity unlike any other – and it is in Cornwall. The unconventional futuristic structure takes its name from the remarkable invention of Sir Goldsworthy Gurney who invented the original Bude Light, a wonderful form of illumination in the days of candles and rushlights. It was first installed in London in 1842 as a street light and in 1839 it illuminated the House of Commons properly for the first time.

To honour Sir Goldsworthy and his invention the modern Bude Light, created by Boscastle scculptor Carol Vincent, made its appearance for Millennium year. It is a slender cone madein concrete and incorporates the colours of sand, sea and sky as it stands on a permanent site overlooked by Bude Castle, Sir Goldsworthy's former home.

The Bude Light is a most spectacular sight at night: a paved area around the cone is the zodiac circle, with the sun, moon and planets being represented by coloured lights. Also included are Sirius (the Dog Star) and the constellation Orion. There is also a scattering of lights to represent other stars, and in order to facilitate identification the constellations are named and their star patterns marked with steel studs. Depending on the season, if the weather is suitable and the sky clear, one can see the planets and constellations in the sky above. The 5ft-diameter circle around the cone represents the seashore. A central drain designed as a compass rose is aligned with the cone on true north. Red bricks in the paving also mark the points of the compass and the top of the cone's shadow shows local apparent noon from 22 March to 22 September – and all this in front of Sir Goldsworthy's former home.

This is an extraordinary scientific demonstration which should not be missed by anyone seeking Cornish curiosities, and is a great tribute to a great Cornishman.

10

BUDE

The Storm Tower

Anyone familiar with the Temple of the Winds in Athens will instantly recognise the Storm Tower. It stands firm against the elements on the exposed Compass Point above some of the cruellest rocks on the Cornish coast, which have claimed many ships and lives over the years.

The tower is an octagonal building, the sides of which are turned to the cardinal and intermediate points of the compass, the names of which are carved into the stone at the top. It stands as a landmark for shipping; there was once a flagstaff by it and a red flag used to be hoisted when ships could not enter the harbour because of the tide. The original tower was demolished in July 1881 because the condition of the cliff below it had rendered it unsafe, at which point Sir Thomas Acland had the present building erected further from the cliff edge. Despite the erosion of the clifftops along this section of the coast, expert geologists have confirmed that the tower is not in danger of falling into the Atlantic Ocean.

11   CALLINGTON

Dupath Well

Holy wells abound in Cornwall. No fewer than 150 have been recorded; some have been lovingly restored, others are now little more than a small trickle of water emerging from a hedge. Early man revered them as healing sources or possessing magical powers or, on a more down-to-earth note, the only source of pure water to sustain life.

Dupath Well, just over a mile from Callington town centre, is one of the most attractive in Cornwall; it is also the largest well building in the county. It was built by the Canons of St Germans in about 1510, who had acquired property at Callington in 1432, which included 'Theu Path'. They owned the well until the Dissolution of the Monasteries in 1538. The well had been abandoned for many years until it was rediscovered by the Revd H.M. Rice, a former rector of South Hill, who actually restored it. In 1936 the late Mr A. de C. Glubb of Liskeard purchased the well for £100 from the owner of the land on which it stood, a Mr J. Hicks, and later the Office of Works, now English Heritage, took it over and agreed to preserve it for all time.

The curiosity value of Dupath Well is that its roof is constructed of thick moorstone blocks which are all fitted neatly together without any binding agent, quite a feat of building expertise.

The water of Dupath Well is believed to cure whooping cough. The miraculous spring rises under the east wall of the building and still flows today.

CALLINGTON

The Old Clink

12

A board on the wall surrounding the parish church in the centre of Callington and pointing the way to 'The Old Clink' is intriguing, and visitors may wonder what they will see if they venture through the gate to visit it. The building is unprepossessing but it has a lot of history attached to it – it is a listed building, so worthy of inspection.

The Old Clink was built in 1851 by John Couch John for the sum of £60. It consisted of two cells for the incarceration of drunks or anyone else causing a disturbance of the peace in the town, and they would be held there until they appeared before the magistrate in the morning. It was much in use during the mining boom in the Callington area when the miners 'came to town' to spend some of their hard-earned cash.

In addition to the two-lock up cells the building also had a vestry room where the leading officer and the overseer for the town decided on the distribution of Poor Relief. In 1851 Henry Bullen was appointed second parish-paid constable and he would have been responsible for apprehending those eligible for a night in the clink. In 1866, with the formation of the Cornwall Constabulary, a police station and cells were built in Tavistock Road and the clink was no longer used as a lock-up.

From that time on it had various uses. In 1895 a standpipe, hose and nozzle was put in the vestry in the care of the clerk to the lighting inspector at Liskeard, for use in case of fire. From 1906 the Clink and vestry were used as a store for various parish paraphernalia and between 1980 and 1990 was used by the church as a recycling depot for paper which could be sold to raise funds.

The present owners, Caradon District Council, spent money on the upkeep of the clink and vestry, and as a listed building it will once more become an important building in the town, probably in conjunction with the Tamar Valley National Heritage Site, designated in 2006, when a use will be found for it, perhaps as an office in connection with the administration of the Heritage Site. More than 150 years old, it is still going strong with a modern use.

13

CALLINGTON

The 'Take Off' Stone

A few miles from Callington just west of Newbridge on the Callington–Liskeard road a steep hill branches off to the left. This was originally the main road to Liskeard until a new road avoiding the steep gradient was constructed.

In the days when all traffic on the road was horse drawn, drivers with heavily laden carts and only one horse could hire a horse at the bottom of the hill to be coupled to their own horse and cart and provide two horsepower to get the load up the hill. Once at the top, the second horse was uncoupled and taken back down the hill to await the next load. The spot where this operation took place is marked by a large stone on the verge, with the words 'Take Off' carved on it, a reminder of the days when road traffic was just as hazardous as it is now but in a very different way. Incidentally, the old road emerges not far from the Take Off stone on to today's main road.

CAMELFORD

The Camel Weathervane

14

Weathervanes come in various shapes and sizes, but if you are in Cornwall and a town that just cries out for something appropriate, well, why waste the opportunity to have something unique?

The weathervane on the clock tower of the Town Hall in Camelford is – you've guessed it – a camel, and probably the only one of its kind in the country. Moreover, the large local Sir James Smith's School badge also incorporates a camel. Actually, the name has nothing to do with the animal. The word is thought to derive from 'cam' (crooked), and 'alan' (beautiful) and 'ford'. Thus it started off as Camalanford and in the course of time got contracted to Camelford.

The Town Hall, right in the centre of the main street (Fore Street), although not large is rather handsome. It was built by the Duke of Bedford over the old Market House in 1806, with a cupola holding two bells, and a double outside staircase leading from Chapel Street to the upper chamber, which has some good coloured glass in the elegant main window. The upper chamber has now become the town library and one of the bells can be seen at the ground-floor entrance.

15

CAWSAND

The Boundary Symbol

This is a tricky one because it marks the boundary of two counties right in the middle of town.

On the wall of a house in narrow Garrett Street, Cawsand, is a strange-looking stone symbol rather like a starfish on top of a pillar. It marks the dividing line between the twin villages of Kingsand and Cawsand. Until 1941 it marked the boundary between the parishes of Maker and Rame, but well over 100 years before that it marked the boundary between Devon and Cornwall. Apparently the boundary line followed a stream behind the Halfway House Inn (which is opposite the house with the boundary symbol) for a short distance, then a hedge line which led up above Coombe Park and a farm and over a hill to Treninnow. Then the stream took over again as the boundary until it reached Millbrook.

Boundaries are always difficult to define, but we are assured that this one divided Devon and Cornwall. These far from straight lines are probably a series of property boundaries; landowners would have known whether their land was in Devon or Cornwall.

The map makers must have had to be very careful in those days but an old map of 1765 does show a rather confusing 'Part of Devon' which appears to show the boundary cutting through the middle of Cawsand.

ST CLEMENT

A 'Third-hand' Gravestone

16

St Clement is a small village near Truro. Its claim to fame is a stone near the church porch which appears to have been used twice as a post-Roman gravestone before being partially converted into a wheel-headed Celtic cross.

It is known as the Ignioc Stone as it is dedicated to Igniocus Vitalis, son of Torricus. It also has an inscription in Ogham, the strange Celtic alphabet which consists of strokes or lines, so it appears to have been reused as subsequent memorials.

The church itself is fourteenth century but was rebuilt in 1865 when restoration was the key word for Cornish church spoliation.

17

CORNWALL

The Cornish Gorseth

On the first Saturday in September the Bards of the Cornish Gorseth gather at a different historical site each year for their open Gorseth, a spectacle witnessed by hundreds of people, many travelling very long distances to be there.

The Cornish Gorseth was inaugurated on 21 September 1928 as what could be described as an offshoot of the Welsh Gorsedd, although it is an entirely autonomous organisation, and while enjoying close links with the Welsh Gorsedd is in no way tied to it. It was formed to 'guard and enhance all that is Cornish in our way of life', to repeat the description

given by Mr Hugh Miners, a former Grand Bard, in his book *Gorseth Kernow – The First Fifty Years*. The Gorseth has as its leader a Grand Bard and there is also a Deputy Grand Bard. All other members hold the rank of Bard.

It is a great honour to be elected to bardship, which is bestowed upon persons in recognition of their contribution to the cultural life of Cornwall in many spheres: it may be outstanding service in music, in literature, in historical research, art or public life of value to the Cornish nation, and in more recent years has been awarded to those attaining proficiency in the Cornish language, after stringent examinations have been passed.

All members of the Gorseth wear the sky blue robes and headdress (trimmed with black and gold) of the Gorseth Kernow (Cornish Gorseth) based on the style of the Roman toga, and all bards take a Cornish bardic name which is bestowed on them at their initiation by the grand bard. Each bard selects his or her own bardic name which is applicable to them; some like to honour the parish, village or town of their birth as 'Son of . . .' or 'Daughter of . . .', while others choose a name applicable to their nomination as a bard. My bardic name, conferred in 1980, is Scryfer Weryn – Writer of Werrington (home parish).

At the Gorseth ceremony the bards swear an oath of fealty to Cornwall and call 'Cres' (peace). The symbol of the Gorseth is the Awen (Cornish for 'inspiration'), a representation of three rays from Heaven, which denote the power of the Father, the wisdom of the Son and the goodness of the Holy Spirit. Every bard is entitled to wear a miniature version of this symbol as a tie or lapel pin. The Gorseth Kernow's open Gorseth is now held on the first Saturday of September at a different venue each year. It is usually attended by representatives of the Welsh Gorsedd (emerald green robes) and the Breton Gorsedd (white robes) and Cornish bards may attend their open ceremonies too, as part of the wider Celtic community.

18 CORNWALL

Cornish Hedges

Cornish hedges are a law unto themselves; they are distinctive and quite different from hedges you will see in other parts of Britain. Basically a Cornish hedge is two granite walls filled with tightly packed earth, but there are variations in the way the stones are laid.

Although I am not qualified to explain the technicalities of building a Cornish hedge, which is a very skilled and specialised craft, there is no lovelier sight than a Cornish hedge topped by wild flowers which have colonised it. The selection of each individual stone in building the hedge is an art in itself and stones often have to be trimmed or dressed to fit tightly together. The biggest stones go at the base and the walls taper slightly as they progress upwards. Walls can be of granite or slate or whatever stone is available locally. The tool used for the excavation at the base and then the earth filling is the long-handled Cornish shovel, which to the uninitiated may look like a cumbersome and unmanageable tool but is actually perfectly balanced and ideal for the job. To see a Cornish shovel being used in the way intended is a joy to watch. It looks so effortless, but the skill of the handler is paramount.

It was gratifying recently to see a Cornish hedge being constructed at the entrance to a new housing development in north Cornwall and being built by young men with an obvious excellent grounding in the skill, proving that one of our native crafts is still alive and well. A good Cornish hedge will last for ever; if a collapsed one is seen it was not constructed properly in the first place.

DAVIDSTOW

The Cornish Bagpiper

'Behold! I Tell You a Mystery' is the title of the opening chapter in bagpipe expert Harry Woodhouse's book *Cornish Bagpipes – Fact or Fiction*. In his book Mr Woodhouse provides evidence that the Cornish bagpipe did exist and further proof of that can be obtained by visiting Davidstow or Altarnun churches, both of which have sixteenth-century bench ends with carvings of a man playing bagpipes of the Cornish variety.

We may tend to think of bagpipes as associated with such events as the Edinburgh Tattoo or Scottish evenings in hotels, but there is far more to these ancient instruments than the skirl of the Scottish pipes. For one thing, the Cornish bagpipe is a smaller and gentler instrument. Although the technique is the same the Cornish bagpipe varies in appearance. Mr Woodhouse's book has a photograph of three modern-day players, each with his own distinctive instrument.

The bagpipers depicted on the Davidstow and Altarnun bench ends play pipes slightly different from each other. There is also a carving on the handsomely carved exterior of St Mary Magdalene Church in Launceston which depicts fifteenth-century minstrels with their instruments, one of them being the Cornish bagpipe. Unfortunately, in the last decade these carvings have been so badly affected by pollution in the air that they are now almost unrecognisable.

If anyone is prepared to crane their neck they can see a comparatively modern bagpiper in the fine church at St Columb Major on a roof boss dating from 1903 beneath the restored medieval church roof, which was in great danger from dry rot. This bagpiper is in the form of an angel, elaborately attired in a red robe with gold trimming, and playing the Cornish bagpipe. Because this is a newer carving it is easier to see the type of instrument being played.

A Cornish bagpiper playing his own set of pipes always leads the procession of bards at the Cornish Gorseth every September when they walk to an appointed historic site to perform their traditional rites.

20 | DAVIDSTOW

A Moorland Mystery

On a patch of marshy ground at the foot of Rough Tor on Bodmin Moor a poignant memorial stands alone and isolated, the only clue to its existence in this remote spot being the inscription on it. The words read 'In memory of Charlotte Dymond who was murdered by Matthew Weeks Sunday April 14 1884'. The memorial was erected by public subscription close to the spot where Charlotte's body was found.

But was Charlotte murdered? She was a servant on a Bodmin Moor farm and was 18 years old at the time of her death. Two labourers were also employed at the farm and Matthew Weeks was one of them.

It was there that Matthew and Charlotte met and formed a relationship, although Charlotte was reputed to be flirtatious and interested in an older man called Thomas Prout. When Charlotte disappeared from Penhale Farm she was assumed to be with Prout.

A number of people claimed to have seen Charlotte walking with Weeks towards Roughtor Ford on 14 April and Charlotte had told her employer that she would not be back to milk the cows that evening. It was near the ford that Charlotte's body was found some days later. On the 14th Weeks returned to Penhale Farm and insisted that he did not know where Charlotte was or where she had gone.

Several incriminating features linked Weeks with Charlotte's disappearance, one being that Charlotte was known to be somewhat promiscuous. Charlotte's body was found on the moor. Her throat had been cut but no weapon was ever found. Suicide was one explanation at the time. Weeks was arrested and remanded in custody on 25 April. He vehemently denied murder, but when he was brought to trial the jury unanimously convicted him of the crime and he was hanged at Bodmin Jail and buried within the confines of the prison.

Charlotte is buried in Davidstow churchyard, her last resting place marked only by a small slate slab set into the ground and bearing her name.

The story of Charlotte Dymond is to this day a matter of conjecture. There are still those who believe it was suicide and that Weeks was innocent. Others are convinced it was murder and that Weeks was responsible. Some even think Prout was the culprit. Everyone can make up their own minds, since at Bodmin's Shire Hall 'The Charlotte Dymond Experience' has been created, enabling visitors to sit through a virtual reconstruction of the trial and decide for themselves what actually happened. However, it is most unlikely that the true answer will ever be known.

DELABOLE

21

The Bettle and Chisel

As they pass through Delabole, many people who are strangers to the area will see the hanging sign for the Bettle and Chisel Inn and will wonder just what the name means. Everyone in Delabole and for miles around knows that bettles and chisels are vital tools used in the splitting of slate, and Delabole is home to one of the biggest slate quarries in the country, if not in the world. Delabole slates have been quarried and worked for generations. When thick slices of slate have to be split into thin ones for roofing slates the bettle and chisel was used. The skilled worker sits at a bench with a slab of slate between his knees and with the chisel splits it into thin slices; the bettle is the type of mallet which hits the chisel.

Slate splitting is a highly skilled occupation which takes years to perfect and at Delabole it is still all done by hand. In some large quarries elsewhere slates are split by machine, so Delabole could well be unique.

Certainly the name of the public house is unique – there is not another in Cornwall, nor, as far as is known, anywhere else. Incidentally, the Bettle and Chisel was known as the Commercial Inn until the outbreak of the Second World War, but there have never been any regrets expressed at the name change.

ST ENDELLION

22

Ringers' Board

Campanology – the art of bell-ringing – is very popular in many Cornish parishes and an absorbing hobby for countless people. It is a skill which even has its own national magazine, as there is far more to it than just pulling a rope and tolling a bell. Complicated change ringing can take years to perfect and even the handling of the bell rope is a knack which has to be learned.

In past times it was not so much the ability of the ringers but their behaviour which was most important. A bell-ringer in church had to toe the line or he would soon be out. This is illustrated by an eighteenth-century board fixed to the wall of the belfry in St Endellion church. It is signed 'John Daw – John Volkin Church-wardens' and very plainly lays down the rules:

I ring the quick to Church the dead to grave.
Good is our use such image let us have.
Who here therefore doth damn, or curse, or swear
Or strike in quarrel, tho' no blood appear
or wear his hat or such or turns a bell,
or any make a noise to mar a peal;
shall six-pence pay for each and every crime.
He'll fear to offend (perhaps) another time,
and since bells are a modell recreation:
let's rise and ring and fall to admiration.

Such rule boards may be seen in a few other towns and young ringers today, joining a team for the first time, are advised to read, learn and inwardly digest the rules because etiquette in the bell tower is as important today as it was all those years ago.

ST ERTH

The Sand Pits

23

There is not much to be seen above ground now, but in times past the sand pits at St Erth were an invaluable contribution to the Industrial Revolution and to industry and craftsmen for many years after that. Now the area of the pits is overgrown with vegetation and is a haven for wildlife. It is managed by Cornwall Wildlife Trust, and because of its important past it is classed as a Special Site of Geological Scientific Interest.

Many people living today still remember the pits being worked, as they continued to be a valuable source of their special type of sand right up to 1950. The famous St Ives potter Bernard Leach used the sand from the pits in his work and Harvey's Foundry at Hayle used it as a mould for casting components. In 1997 fossil sea shells from Pliocene shell beds were found in perfect condition there, causing excitement in the realms of geological research and study.

The sand from the pits is unique as each grain is coated with a fine film of clay, which is found only at St Erth and in very small quantities at Beacon Pit, St Agnes. It was invaluable (and still is) in the metal-casting process, although doubtless such material is now imported from sources abroad.

The pits are fenced off and carefully managed, but an application for permission to visit them may be made to the Cornwall Wildlife Trust.

ST EWE

24

The Hangman's Tree

Public hangings were at one time a spectacle not to be missed, a form of entertainment which brought people scurrying to the appointed place. They were watched with interest and bloodthirsty fascination. The hanging of petty criminals was an all too common occurrence, because offenders could be hanged for such 'minor' crimes as sheep stealing.

In the hamlet of Penglugla, in St Ewe parish, is a living reminder of those somewhat barbaric times. The Hangman's Tree, known by that name for centuries, stands just behind the village postbox. It was on this tree that many an unfortunate miscreant was 'strung up' in days gone by. Beyond the hedge behind the tree is a small patch of rough, uncared for ground, said to have been the burial place of the hanged. It certainly is a rather gloomy, sad place.

ST EWE

The Tremayne Arms

In St Ewe church is a slate memorial to the Tremayne family who lived at Heligan (pronounced Hel-ig-an) and which includes a carving of the Tremayne family arms; this resembles the triskelion symbol of the Isle of Man, the 'Three Legs of Man', which gives rise to the Island's motto 'It will stand wherever you may throw it', or in modern parlance 'whichever way you throw me I stand'. The Manx symbol is believed to have originated from Sicily as far back as the eleventh century.

However, although the Cornish and the Manx are fellow Celts, that is where the connection with the Tremayne family ends, for the carving on the Tremayne memorial does not depict legs, but three arms with clenched hands; they are actually a pun – 'Tremayne' – in Norman French, *trés mains*, three hands – and is a concoction of the College of Heralds and the family at a time when it was fashionable to hint at French origins and the possibility that the family arrived with William the Conquerer. The surname actually derived from a Cornish place-name, Tremayne, a farmstead still in the parish of St Mawgan in Meneage. The Tremaynes were at Heligan for 400 years, but in about 1970 the last of the family to own it started converting the great house into twenty-two flats. The extensive gardens are now a tourist attraction known as the Lost Gardens of Heligan, and have been developed as a large garden complex.

26

FALMOUTH

Jacob's Ladder

What do you do when you want to get from one level of your town to another without following a long circuitous route? Why, you build a staircase, of course. And this is just what Jacob Hamblyn did in the eighteenth century.

Mr Hamblyn was a well-known and influential resident in the town and when in 1791 a Wesleyan chapel was built Mr Hamblyn foresaw that many would-be worshippers would be unable to reach the chapel easily. So he had 111 granite steps built from the The Moor in the centre of Falmouth to the area above on the very high ground.

It soon became known as Jacob's Ladder and is used to this day, squeezed between two buildings in the busy hub of the town and leading from The Moor to Vernon Place, providing a short cut for those able to accept its challenge. It is quite common to see intrigued holidaymakers, attracted by this unusual steep flight of steps, starting the stiff climb but glancing upwards and seeing how much further they will have to go to reach the top, losing heart and turning back!

FALMOUTH

The Queen's Pipe

27

In days gone by the busy port of Falmouth was a mecca for smugglers, and a strange reminder of those rip-roaring days can still be seen. At the end of the valley at Custom House Quay, close to the waterfront, a curious-looking structure stands out. It is known as the Queen's Tobacco Pipe, or as some called it, the King's Tobacco Pipe, as the reigning monarch changed. It was built as an incinerator for the vast quantity of smuggled tobacco whichwas being brought into the port. At one time Falmouth had a thriving tobacco smuggling 'industry'. Eventually the authorities clamped down on the trade with all the illicit 'weed' going up in smoke in the pipe.

The trade in tobacco gradually died out and so did the use of the pipe. In later years the small amounts of smuggled tobacco seized were handed on to the workhouse for the men there to enjoy quite legitimately. But that custom, too, died out many years ago and now tourists make a special detour off the main street to see the pipe.

28

FALMOUTH

The Oldest Shop Front

What is probably the oldest existing shop front in Cornwall is that of 54 Church Street, Falmouth. The Grade II listed property dates back to about 1780 and the bow-fronted shop window was created in the early nineteenth century.

English Heritage describes the premises as 'an extremely fine example of an early 19th century shop front of outstanding quality in a national context and comparable to the best examples of shop fronts in London and other fashionable provincial towns'.

The shop itself had a central spiral staircase leading to a lower-ground floor.

It certainly stands out among all the modern shop fronts in the town. When the building was erected Falmouth was a very busy and prosperous sea port attracting trade from all over the world.

FOWEY

Chain Defences

29

In the fifteenth century Cornwall was vulnerable to attack and all sorts of ingenious forms of defences were put in place to deter the enemy.

During the reign of Edward IV (1461–83) the harbour and town of Fowey were wide open to attack, so a small castle was built on a rocky outcrop by the water's edge, matched by another in Polruan, on the other side of Fowey harbour.

These blockhouses were chain towers. A heavy chain was laid on the sea bed between the two buildings which could be raised in order to protect the harbour entrance from attack, particularly from the French. They prevented any ships from entering.

Only fourteen such defences were built in Britain and the one at Fowey is the oldest. It is situated just below a modern dwelling known as Castleruan and can be seen from the sea or the other side of the harbour. It is now in ruins but just enough of it remains to show that it was manned by a garrison, always alert and prepared to raise the chain whenever necessary, and it can be seen that it was quite a substantial building in its time. It is now private property, part of the grounds of Castleruan.

30

ST GERMANS

Dando and His Dogs

The imposing church of St Germans with its magnificent Norman doorway has many items of interest within it but one in particular is curious. It is a medieval misericord which illustrates a local legend.

Misericords are bracketed projections on the underside of the seats of choir stalls, to afford rest to a person standing for a long time when the seat is folded up. In medieval times when services were long and drawn out and in the monasteries when monks were often required to stand for substantial periods, those who were elderly or infirm found the misericord a lifesaver, as they could partially sit when standing became too much for them.

Misericords were often carved with fanciful designs and the one at St Germans is no exception. Incidentally, it is the only part which remains of the furnishings of the priors' choir at St Germans, which was demolished soon after the Dissolution of the Monasteries. The legend of Dando is gruesome. He was a monk at St Germans Friary who was not faithful to his vows was interested only in imbibing wine and hunting for game, to such an extent that he totally neglected his religious duties, not even observing Sundays.

According to the legend, one Sunday he was out hunting and drinking large quantities of wine. He called for more wine to be brought and when told there was none left he shouted 'Get it from Hell as there is none left on earth'. At that moment, it was said, a stranger stepped forward and offered Dando his flask, from which the monk drank greedily, emptying the flask. Immediately he was transformed, behaving like a raging bull. He and the stranger fought fiercely over the game they had hunted and Dando fell from his horse. The stranger jumped into Dando's saddle and dragged Dando up in front of him, whipping the horse down the hill at a mad gallop, plunging into the River Lynher. Hunters, horse and hounds were never seen again. The story goes that Dando's hunting companions were also transformed, many of them going to live in the priory and devoting their lives to the service of God and the church. Others made rich gifts to the priory as thanks for their deliverance from Dando's fate.

The misericord at St Germans commemorates this legend. On it Dando is shown with his hounds, carrying the game he had bagged on the stock of his crossbow, which rests on his shoulder. It is truly a unique carving for a church decoration.

GERMOE

Text Boards

31

Little Germoe church, lying in a hollow at the foot of Tregonning Hill, has several odd features, one of which is a collection of wooden message boards, only two of which now remain. We are told that at one time the rough stone walls were covered by these boards, but of the two that remain the heart-shaped one is in remarkably good condition for its age, considering that it is dated 1724.

It is inscribed in bold lettering 'Remember the Poor'. Assuming that everyone in the congregation could read in those days (possibly a bit unlikely) these little messages ensured that all members of the congregation kept 'on the straight and narrow' and followed their Christian duties. This is also a reminder that in the past churches provided poor relief as well as maintaining their fabric, so the contents of

the offertory plate or bag helped with that relief; thus the congregation would be well aware of the need to give.

GUNWALLOE

32

The Bell Tower

The church of St Winwaloe at Gunwalloe, 'the Church of the Storms', was founded by St Winwaloe who had a cell on the site in the shelter of Castle Hill, where there is an Iron Age castle earthwork. The most unusual thing about the church is the West Tower, the bell tower, which is totally detached from the church and is believed to date from about the thirteenth century. It is built in a cave-hermitage 14ft away from the church and has stood thus for some 600 years. Part of its sides are formed out of the rock to which it clings very firmly. The bell tower has a pyramid-shaped roof which was restored in 1938 and according to the church leaflet its three medieval bells were recast in 1926 to make a chime of six, rung by hand carillon.

Gunwalloe church is close to Dollar Cove, known at one time as 'the treasure seeker's paradise' because in 1743 a Spanish ship carrying 2½ tons of gold 'pillar' dollars was wrecked there; it is believed that the coins are still buried in the sand of the cove.

Lots of people have dug in the sand but there have not been reports of any big finds – however, hope springs eternal and when visiting the cove it is difficult to resist the temptation to scrape away at the sand just in case!

GWENNAP

Preaching Pits

33

When mining in Cornwall was in its heyday a great religious upheaval was also taking place. In 1743 the arrival of John Wesley brought Methodism to the county. He crossed what he described as 'the first great pathless moor' (Bodmin Moor) on his first visit. He subsequently travelled the roads and tracks throughout the county bringing his religious beliefs to thousands of people who had perhaps never before bothered with religion, but became what were then known as Wesleyans. There were a few splinter groups – the Primitive Methodists, the Bible Christians, the United Methodist Free Churches, and so on – but all were teaching Methodism much as Wesley was doing, each with its own slight variation.

The religious fervour was tremendous and one Cornish curiosity which arose from this was the preaching pits. As mines were worked out and abandoned they were filled up, and the sunken floors provided amphitheatres where Wesley and others could preach the gospel. The largest and most famous of these is at Gwennap where thousands

of people gathered to hear John Wesley preach. The great grassed amphitheatre is over 300yds in circumference and has grassy tiers of seats to accommodate those who flocked there. It has remarkable acoustic properties, and even if there had been microphones in those days there would have been no need for them: everyone could hear what was being said and sung.

Every Whitsun, to this day, thousands of Methodists gather at Gwennap Pit, and two stone pillars mark the spot from which Wesley preached, known as Wesley's pulpit.

There is a smaller but equally handsome pit at Indian Queens and even smaller ones at St Newlyn East and Whitemoor, near St Austell.

There was a great expansion of Cornish Methodism after Wesley died and to attend a service at Gwennap Pit on Wesley Day is an unforgettable experience. All the pits are kept in good order and can be easily visited.

GWITHIAN

The Thatched Chapel

34

Thatched Methodist chapels are very rare and the one at Gwithian has an added distinction in that it is still in use today. It is a pretty little whitewashed building which looks more like a cottage than a place of worship and it has another claim to posterity being, in 1959, the first Methodist chapel to be grant aided by the Cornwall Historic Churches Trust, which up until then had only provided help to Anglican churches.

Another former thatched chapel, Roseworthy in Gwinear, has now been converted into a dwelling house and even boasts a thatched garage to match.

35

HAYLE

Black Bricks

People visiting Hayle for the first time are often surprised to see garden walls and walls of houses and buildings constructed with large shiny black bricks almost like glass, very different from the usual red or beige bricks to which they are accustomed. This is one of the peculiarities of being in the heart of a former copper-mining area.

By the 1830s Cornwall was the world's leading producer of copper. In Hayle a large quay was constructed to service the industry. Black slag was the by-product or waste material from the copper smelting process and instead of allowing it to go to waste it was moulded into large bricks, often up to 2cwt each, depending on the use to which they were to be put. These curious bricks were known locally as Scoria Blocks and were sold at 9d for twenty, but miners had free access to as many as they wanted to build their own homes. The blocks take their name from the Greek word skoria (refuse), applied to the refuse of fused metals, and even gave their name to Scorrier near Redruth, a place at one time in the very heart of the Redruth–Camborne mining area.

The black bricks can be seen everywhere in Hayle and Phillack and there was even a bridge built of them and known as the Black Bridge; they were even incorporated in the walls of Phillack church. Although a novelty today, the black bricks were once everyday objects to the inhabitants of the Cornish copper-mining districts.

HELSTON

Loe Pool

Loe Pool is the largest lake in Cornwall, 7 miles in circumference and according to Tennyson the place where Sir Bedivere threw the sword Excalibur. It is mysterious, almost sinister, especially in stormy weather, and it is unique, with a bar of gravel and flint separating it from the sea; in the words of a former poet laureate, probably John Betjeman, 'A sort of Chesil beach with a fresh water lagoon behind it'.

The setting on the Penrose estate is idyllic, with the steeply wooded sides rising above the pool, but an old superstition says that it claims a visitor every seven years, a rather chilling thought when one is walking the footpath which skirts it.

HELSTON

The Wheelbarrow Path

37

In the days before quad bikes and other modern means of moving loads, wheelbarrows were a must for transporting light goods. Unlike today's lightweight implement, Victorian wheelbarrows were heavy, solid affairs of stout wood, often unwieldy for those unaccustomed to handling them; on hills they could be lethal if heavily laden.

In order to make passage easier for wheelbarrow users Helston had a special path for them on the hill going down to the pipe well. Heavy granite stones the width of the path were sunk into the ground at regular intervals, like railway sleepers. These would inhibit the free passage of wheelbarrows by preventing them from running away with the handler on downhill runs and would allow barrows to be rested to give the handler a short respite when being pushed uphill. The steps are still there today although it is unlikely they are used very often for their original purpose. My mother remembered them being used regularly when she was a small child at the end of the nineteenth century.

THE ISLES OF SCILLY

38

A Lost Community

The beautiful Isles of Scilly comprise fifty uninhabited islands as well as the few larger and well-known inhabited ones which attract visitors from all over the world. One of those uninhabited islands has an intriguing past and efforts are now being made to unravel its many secrets.

The island of Samson, all 95 acres of it, the largest of the uninhabited islands, has not been occupied for more than 160 years. Records show that one family was living on Samson as far back as 1669; by 1794 there were six houses and thirty people living there and by 1829 thirty-six people had their homes on the island. Then in 1855 the last ten residents were ordered to leave, but they left behind them a legacy which is now being explored. Nineteen ruined buildings remain to remind us of those last residents, who doubtless suffered hardship and great sadness when they had to leave their idyllic island home. The whole island is a Scheduled Ancient Monument and a Site of Special Scientific Interest because it is totally unspoilt. In 2006 a project got under way to preserve the remains of the historic buildings; conservation work will use traditional materials and rampant vegetation will be controlled and managed.

It is possible to visit Samson on occasional boat trips from the inhabited islands and volunteers are being sought to assist in the project which will, it is hoped, throw light at last on the story of a historic island community. The sad, deserted island will live again and be preserved for posterity.

ST JUST-IN-PENWITH

39

The Men-an-Tol

Ancient stones and prehistoric monuments abound in Cornwall. All had some particular significance but the actual purpose of some of them will never be known despite all the research by the finest experts in the land; the stones retain the secrets of their origins. Standing stones (menhirs), stone rows and circles, quoits (burial chambers, originally grassed over) and holed stones all meant a great deal to ancient man and have over the years acquired their own legends and superstitions. Some we do know were tombs, others had some form of religious significance, but many more are still open to conjecture.

The finest of the holed stones is the Men-an-Tol on the moors of west Penwith, the furthest corner of the county. Men-an-Tol actually means 'the holed stone', one of those things which is just another little quirk of Cornishness that makes the county special and different.

The whole structure consists of two upright stones with a round stone of approximately 2ft in diameter standing upright between them with a hole 2ft in circumference through the centre. Some experts think it was originally the entrance stone to a burial chamber such as the nearby Lanyon Quoit, but S.P.B. Mais in his book *The Cornish Riviera* says that astronomers claim holed stones were used for sighting the sunrise. A superstition existing to this day and still believed by many is that the stone has healing powers and that passing a child (or anyone for that matter, if they can manage it) through the hole will cure them of rickets, scrofula and spinal disease, although the drawback is that they are supposed to be naked for the powers to work.

40

ST JUST IN PENWITH

The Plain an Gwarry

There is a very long tradition of outdoor theatre in Cornwall but its origins are somewhat shrouded in mystery. There is evidence that the pagan Celts, long before the arrival of the Romans, used open-air sites for their religious ceremonies and it is believed that these involved dancing in some form. However, historical evidence about such places dates from a period when Cornwall had been Christian for centuries, and one school of thought is that Christian drama had its roots in dramatised readings of The Passion during Lent and Easter. Cornwall did have its own Passion play, the Ordinalia, thought to have been a three-day event rather like the famous Oberammergau Passion play in Austria, and the original stage directions for this event show it taking place in the open air in a circular 'playing place'.

The open air amphitheatre of Plain an Gwarry in the centre of St Just in Penwith, one of several in Cornwall, was possibly the largest and the best known. Here would have been performed miracle plays, spoken in the original Cornish language and attended by people from miles around, who would make their way to this venue just as today people from all over the county converge on the annual Royal Cornwall Show.

In some parts of Britain religious plays were forbidden for being superstitious, but the Cornish, ever defiant and ever 'different', continued with theirs, which grew in popularity. The manuscript of the most recent Cornish play was copied in 1611, five years before the death of William Shakespeare, but the date of the last Cornish performance is not known.

The Plain an Gwarry has in modern times seen displays of Cornish wrestling and dancing, and the Cornish Gorseth has been held in it. It is an ideal setting for all these events (incidentally there is a village near St Austell, called Playing Place).

There are those who think that the coming of John Wesley sounded the death knell of such frivolous pursuits which took place in the aptly named 'playing places', although one cannot imagine the independent Cornish people allowing even their religious beliefs to interfere with their fun.

KILKHAMPTON

41

The Hyssop Bench End

On reflection, it is surprising the subjects the medieval craftsmen chose to carve on church bench ends in Cornwall. Some of them are described in this book – corn dollies, a Cornish bagpiper, the mermaid of Zennor – and now another, hyssop, depicted on a bench end in Kilkhampton church.

King Solomon was aware of the value of moss, for we learn from the Bible that he spoke of 'trees from the cedar tree that is in Lebanon, even unto the hyssop that springeth out of the wall'. Eminent botanists have identified the hyssop as a tiny moss which still grows even today on the ancient walls of Jerusalem.

We may not be knowledgeable about the unusual plant growth, but whoever carved the medieval bench ends in Kilkhampton church knew all about it because the church guide book informs us that one of the bench ends depicts 'hyssop growing on reeds'. Sure enough, on one of the bench ends is a carving of what looks like sticks with little bumps on them – the medieval carver's interpretation of moss growing on reeds.

42 LAUNCESTON

Eagle House

Eagle House is a beautiful Georgian building dating from the eighteenth century which has an interesting and unusual history. It is situated in Castle Street, described by the former Poet Laureate John Betjeman as 'the finest Georgian street in Cornwall'. Unfortunately, that was before the council in its wisdom or otherwise decided to demolish some of the early buildings and erect a block of modern flats instead.

The house was built in the eighteenth century by Corydon Carpenter, a former mayor of the town and pillar of the community at the time and to whom there is a glowing epitaph on a memorial tablet in St Mary Magdalene's Church, although it has long been rumoured that he wrote it himself before his demise. From all accounts he was a character with an eye to the main chance.

Carpenter was said to have built the house after winning £10,000 in a lottery which enabled him to marry the lady he had been courting and take up residence with her in a fabulous new property. However, he did not endear himself to the local residents when he was said to have purloined stone from the north gate of the castle, over which there was formerly a gaoler's residence, thus leaving the structure in ruins.

On top of Eagle House is an allegorical figure somewhat resembling Britannia. Local children were always told (and implicitly believed until more sophisticated times) that when the figure heard St Mary's Church clock strike thirteen it would descend from its perch and walk up the hill to the church. Bitter disappointment often ensued when nothing happened – as this writer can testify!

Eagle House is now a hotel which upholds the standards set in its days when it was a private dwelling.

LAUNCESTON

St Mary Magdalene's Church

43

The parish church of St Mary Magdalene in the centre of Launceston has the finest carved exterior of any church in the British Isles. The present church is said to be the third dedicated to St Mary Magdalene on the same site and was dedicated on 18 June 1524.

The church was built by Henry Trecarrell of Lezant, the second of the three manorial lords of Lezant. There are varying legends about Trecarrell's intention in building the church. It is agreed that it was motivated by a family tragedy but versions of that tragedy vary. One is that Trecarrell's infant son drowned in bath water and that Trecarrell was so distraught that instead of building himself a magnificent new manor house he built the church instead. Since Trecarrell had only three daughters and no son that version can be dismissed. Another, and more likely, version is that the youngest of Trecarrell's daughters was seduced by the son of a neighbouring landowner, to whom

she bore a son and that, as a result of this shame being brought on the Trecarrell family, Henry built the church as a penance, an expected and accepted custom in those far-off days. Trecarrell himself is often referred to locally as Sir Henry Trecarrell, but although holding high office under both the government and the Duchy he was not knighted, and remained Henry Trecarrell Esquire, buried at Lezant. This omission (as some see it) could be attributed to the fact that he had suffered a penance. We shall never know for sure.

The carvings in the very hard granite are remarkable and they stretch around the entire exterior of the church, as elaborate at the back as in the front. These all merit inspection, beginning with the porch which shows flower and fruit heads of the nardus and pomegranate from which was made the spikenard ointment with which Mary Magdalene anointed Christ's feet. Above the main door is carved a shield bearing the arms of Trecarrell and Kelway (his wife). These occur frequently on separate panels on different parts of the walls, but strangely the arms of the wife predominate. Also over the porch are carvings of St Martin of Tours sharing his cloak with the beggar and St George slaying the dragon, and on each side of the porch and on the northern and southern wall windows is the ostrich plume borne over the arms of the Dukes of Cornwall.

Shields are presented supported by bears, an eagle and a pelican and the early Launceston archives show that such animals and birds were occasionally brought to the town as examples for the sculptors. The most famous sculpture is below the east window and is of St Mary Magdalene reclining beside her pot of spikenard ointment, with behind her the arms of St Germans Priory. An old local superstition has it that if a stone or a small coin is thrown and remains on the back of the figure it will bring luck to the thrower.

Above the east window is a carving of the arms of King Henry VIII, a wise form of insurance because to cause Henry VIII displeasure often ended in beheading. Henry had ordered that the royal arms should be attached to the walls of every parish church and the Launceston ones are believed to be the only specimen in Cornwall wrought in stone. The arms are mostly displayed inside churches.

Also on the east wall are depicted the famous St Mary's minstrels, each with an instrument, who provided music in the church long before the days of organs. Unfortunately, the carvings have been seriously eroded by pollution in the air and many of the instruments are unrecognisable.

The carving which intrigues most people is the inscription. It is interspersed with shields (some bearing arms) which run around the exterior walls of the church above the plinth at the base of the wall. The inscription is in Latin and translates as:

Hail Mary full of grace
The Lord is with thee
The bridegroom loves the bride
Mary chose the best part
O how terrible and fearful is this place
Truly this is no other than the house
of God, and the gate of Heaven.

It is made up of verses of Holy Scripture and a card on sale in the church gives further details.

Only a brief description such as this can be given here of the glories of the exterior of St Mary Magdalene's Church. It has to be seen and carefully examined to fully appreciate the skill of those ancient carvers. It is possible to walk freely around almost the whole exterior of the building.

LAUNCESTON

44

Masonic Gravestone

Gravestones can be fascinating and an are interesting subject to study. Many of the old ones often have enigmatic epitaphs, some epitaphs are amusing and one can speculate on the reason for them being worded as they are.

In the churchyard of St Mary Magdalene's Church in Launceston, close to the public footpath which runs by the east end of the church to what used to be the militiamen's parade ground during the Napoleonic Wars, is what is probably a gravestone unique in its wording. The stone is certainly believed to be unique in Cornwall and possibly in the country. It marks the grave of Richard Criper who died in 1809 and who was quite obviously a dedicated Freemason.

Carved at the top of the gravestone are symbols important to Freemasons – sun, square and compass, etc. The epitaph is really quite remarkable and uses Freemasonry terminology:

Sacred to the memory of Richard Criper who departed this life the
7th day of September 1809 in the 29th year of his age
In full hope of admission to the Grand Celestial Lodge above.
In the Eternal Degree of Bliss and Happiness.

When worthless grandeur to its dust return
No heart-felt grief attends the fable bier:
But when the Friend, the Husband lov'd, we mourn,
Deep is the sorrow, genuine the tear.

Stranger, shoulds't thou approach this hallow'd stone
The merits of the valued dead to seek
Let not the **MYSTIC BROTHERHOOD** alone,
Let those who lov'd him, those who knew him speak.

Oh let them in some pause of anguish say
What Love inspir'd what faith enlarg'd his breast
How soon the unfettered spirit wing'd its way
From earth to heaven, from suffering to be blest.

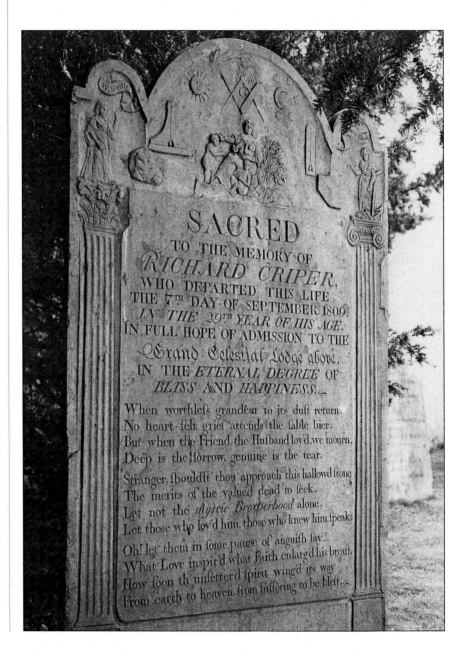

The stone is beautifully carved; all the lettering and symbols are as clear today as they were when they were first cut.

In Werrington churchyard there is another gravestone with Masonic symbols, but the wording does not relate to these in any way.

LAUNCESTON

The Pyper–Wise Monument

45

One of the strangest monuments in any church in Cornwall is in St Mary Magdalene's Church at Launceston. It is an enormous affair and is only a cenotaph because no one is buried beneath it. This strange memorial is unusual because it is attributed to a single-sex couple whose true relationship will never be known.

Monuments to single-sex couples are very uncommon, although there are a few famous examples in the country, notably the seventeenth-century memorial to Sir Thomas Baines and Sir John Finch at Christ College, Cambridge. The Launceston example was erected in the eighteenth century under the terms of the will of Richard Wise, who had been employed by Granville Pyper, grandson of the famous Sir Hugh Pyper, prominent for his support of the Royalist cause during the

Civil War. The monument is designed in two tiers supported by classical marble columns after the style of Inigo Jones and is crowned by busts of Pyper and Wise, bewigged and dignified. Everything about the monument is symbolic; everything has its meaning.

The bond between Pyper and Wise was extremely strong, although only master and servant, and it remained so in death in the form of the elaborate monument in this Launceston church and a memorial tablet in Bath Abbey. What is unusual is that both were erected at the instigation of the servant and not the patron. In his will Wise left the sum of £500 for the building of the memorial in St Mary Magdalene's Church and provided specific instructions concerning the design, but both men are actually buried in Bath. Pyper died there and Wise died in Launceston but left a request that his remains be buried in Bath beside his friend.

The erection of the monument in Launceston caused considerable controversy but it went ahead nevertheless. A large oval tablet incorporated in it carries a lengthy epitaph in Latin, part of which translates: 'As they had been in life of one mind and most closely associated together, so now after death these equally true hearted friends are not divided'. The inscription is obviously intended to give clear indication that friendship and admiration inspired the monument and there is a certain sense of servitude, so admiration and gratitude rather than any other relationship could be assumed.

There are so many contradictory clues about the memorial. A flaming urn as part of the decoration symbolises the mingling of the ashes, reunion after death promised by a common grave. The urn is placed above the earthly level, a popular eighteenth-century interpretation and was a common funerary symbol at that time, but normally reserved for heterosexual relationships. It is perhaps significant that the cartouches of the two deceased are not impaled. The memorial is two tiered, which could imply that Pyper was obviously patron, or perhaps the dominant figure in the relationship, as is the case with other single-sex tombs.

Whatever one chooses to read into this flamboyantly ornate memorial it will forever remain an enigma. It is just another little piece of truly curious Cornwall.

LAUNCESTON

46

The Quarter Jacks

They have wielded their little hammers for well over 300 years and are still going strong. They are the quarter jacks which stand over the clock at the entrance to the Guildhall in Launceston. They are a pair of little blackamoors and known locally as 'The Black Jacks'.

The quarter jacks were carved from oak in 1642 or 1649 (the actual year is not known) and are believed to have been originally on Hexworthy House, a large house a few miles south of Launceston and now turned into apartments. During the Civil War it was the home of Colonel Bennett, a staunch Parliamentarian, and Oliver Cromwell is reputed to have stayed there.

The jacks were probably moved to a site over the old Guildhall that replaced an even earlier one, and stood in The Square, and which was demolished in 1820 to make way for the Butter Market. The jacks then presided over the Butter Market clock but that building was in turn demolished in 1920 to make way for the War Memorial after the First World War. The jacks were moved yet again, to their present position over the Guildhall clock, the third Guildhall in the town having been built in the 1840s. Incidentally, the clock also came from Hexworthy.

The jacks strike every quarter-hour and in less sophisticated days were a great amusement for children who delighted in seeing them 'perform'. Nowadays they are often either unknown or unnoticed, but they have a charming small part in Launceston's history and should be appreciated as a curiosity in their own right.

47 LAUNCESTON

The Reversed 'E'

During the English Civil War feelings and loyalties in Cornwall ran high. The county's involvement was great, with some notable battles being fought on Cornish soil in the north of the county. Those who supported the Royalist cause devised a novel and secret way of showing their allegiance to the Crown.

One easily seen example of this is incorporated in the exterior of St Mary Magdalene's Church in Launceston. Visitors inspecting the magnificent carving on the exterior of the building (including pious sentences in Latin carved into the stone) are often intrigued when following the letters around the church to find on the corner of the east end one letter which does not look quite right. On inspection it can be seen that one stone has at some time been removed and replaced by another. The replacement itself is curious because it appears to show a letter 'E' carved the wrong way around. Who caused this unusual stone to be placed long after the church was built will never be known but it is of great significance.

During the Civil War landowners and local gentry in their fine manor houses and mansions mainly supported the Royalist cause, and to demonstrate that allegiance they had a stone carved with a reverse 'E' built into their properties, sometimes above a main door. Examples can be seen at Werrington Park house, a few miles from Launceston, and at Penfound Manor, near Bude. The one at St Mary's, placed long after

the church was built by Henry Trecarrell, is rather surprising because Launceston came out in favour of the Parliamentarians during the Civil War.

'But why the letter "E?"?' people often ask. 'What is its significance?' The answer is that 'E' stands for Elizabeth. Queen Elizabeth had preserved Protestantism and most of the gentry and well-to-do people at that time staunchly supported that. Consequently, the reversed 'E' indicated that they stood firm for King and Country, supporting the Royalist cause above all others.

LAUNCESTON

Slate Chimney Pots

Castle Street, Launceston was at one time the grandest street in the town with the finest houses and the wealthiest inhabitants. During the Napoleonic Wars, when Launceston was a parole town for French prisoners of war, it was selected for the billeting of naval officer prisoners, the houses being the only ones in the town large enough to accommodate extra residents. The main curiosity in the street is the slate chimney pots. Instead of the usual terracotta the chimney pots each consist of four slates riveted together. They have stood the test of time and are still as sturdy and functional as they were when they were erected. The slates were probably local, possibly from the now long-defunct Barricadoes Quarry to the north of the town.

Slate was quarried locally at several locations. The quarry at Yeolmbridge, 2 miles north of the town, was said to yield particularly fine slate; it was, in fact, reputed to be of even superior quality to that from the famous Delabole Quarry. However, Yeolmbridge Quarry closed down quite suddenly in the early 1930s after having been in operation since the eighteenth century. It was unexpectedly discovered that bedrock had been reached and there was nothing further of value to be obtained from the site. (The former slate quarry at Hurdon, south of the town, used to yield specimens of an unusual fossil coral species.)

Slate chimney pots were at one time quite common in north Cornwall, which was not surprising given the amount of slate being quarried in the area, but the only place apart from Launceston where they can be found is on the Old Post Office at Tintagel, a National Trust property of great antiquity and historical importance.

49

LAUNCESTON

Staddle Stones

You have probably seen staddle stones being used as garden ornaments, but to see them being used for their real purpose is a rare sight. The dictionary definition of the word 'staddle' is 'a support or prop' and that is exactly the purpose of staddle stones. The mushroom-shaped stones (in Cornwall usually of granite) were used as props to form a platform for a granary building to prevent rats getting at the corn. A fine slate-hung granary at Trewithick Farm, Launceston, has its full complement of staddle stones and is still used for its original purpose.

Most Cornish staddle stones are made of granite, but there were earlier slate examples in which both the cap and the post are slate. The slate type has a hole in the middle of the cap which fits down over the post; the granite ones fit on to the post. So desirable are these items today that they are quite often stolen from gardens by thieves who can sell them, again as garden ornaments. There have been a number of prosecutions in recent years for this type of theft.

LAUNCESTON

50

The Trecarrell Portraits

The sumptuously carved exterior of St Mary Magdalene's Church in the centre of the town has been a source of wonder for centuries. Probably thousands of people have gazed upon and admired the plethora of carvings depicting so many different subjects, but there are two that they often miss.

When Henry Trecarrell built the church in the sixteenth century he was so proud of it that he had portraits of himself and his wife carved into the rich decoration and they can be seen flanking the first window on the right as one faces the porch – Henry on the left, his wife on the right. Despite Henry's vanity the portraits are today little known and usually overlooked by both residents and visitors to the town, although doubtless during his lifetime Henry took care to point them out to everyone admiring his church's magnificent edifice!

51 LELANT

Skeleton Gnomon

Slate sundials on churches are quite common in Cornwall and are usually situated above the main doorway. The one at Lelant is much more quirky than the norm. The gnomon (the plate on a sundial which indicates the time of day by its shadow) is in the form of a skeleton holding an hourglass. The skeleton is dressed as a sixteenth-century gentleman complete with headgear.

The church itself was once deemed to have an uncertain future when in 1820 a pessimistic Dean wrote: 'The church must one day be overwhelmed unless the sands are planted with rushes.' Whether they were or not we do not know, but the church is still standing and in regular use.

These days the church is surrounded by a golf course and that, too, appears to be flourishing.

52 ST LEVAN

St Levan's Stone

St Levan's Stone is a dominant feature in the little churchyard in west Cornwall. This enormous boulder has at some time split asunder and thereby hangs a tale. It now appears to be in two almost complete

parts and one cannot visualise the sort of upheaval which caused such a gigantic boulder to split like this. But there is a simple local explanation for it. An age-old legend has it that St Levan always rested on this rock after he had been fishing and one day, exasperated at his poor catch, he hit it with his staff and caused it to crack into two halves. Another version is that he hit it with his fist in a burst of temper. Whichever way he achieved that miracle he followed it up by uttering a dire warning – that when, with panniers astride, a packhorse can walk through St Levan's Stone the world will be done! Another version of the legend is that the Devil cracked the stone one stormy night, pulling it apart, and thus bringing nearer the end of the world.

Whichever story you believe, it is a bit spooky. No attempt has ever been made to interfere with the stone and some local people will swear that the stone has moved further apart in their lifetime. But these days who can provide a packhorse and panniers to test the truth of the story?

LEWANNICK

The Cresset Stone

53

There are only nine cresset stones known to exist in the whole of Britain and one of those is in Cornwall. The cresset stone in Lewannick church is irreplaceable and said to be the best preserved of all of them. Such a circular stone with indentations was used for holding oil, poured into the numerous small depressions in it and used to provide light in the church in medieval times. It could possibly have been mounted on a stone column to provide the maximum lighting for the building.

A disastrous fire in the church in 1890, caused by stove pipes which passed through the roof overheating and setting fire to the roof, almost resulted in the loss of or severe damage to the cresset stone, but thankfully it escaped unscathed and is now back in its rightful place in the church.

Another interesting feature in Lewannick church is a fine Norman font with a complicated maze pattern carved on it, the like of which appears nowhere else on a font, as far as is known.

LINKINHORNE

54

The Darley Oak

Ancient trees are not all that uncommon in Cornwall, but get ready to meet probably the 'daddy' of them all – the Darley Oak in the parish of Linkinhorne, a few miles from Liskeard. The tree is on land which was part of the Dingle estate from as far back as the time of the Black Prince, the first Duke of Cornwall, in the fourteenth century. The estate remained in the Dingle family until sold in 1919.

In his *History of Linkinhorne Parish* written in 1727, author W. Harvey states that 'In the plaisance of the villa stands the great natural curiosity known as the "Darley Oak". It is reasonably supposed to be upwards of 500 years old, it is still healthful and vigorous, annually making shoots and producing acorns'; he adds: 'Darley Oak housed small pleasure parties . . . and was thirty six feet in circumference'. Since then it has been established that the tree is at least 1,000 years old. It was presumably named after Thomas Darley, who was a landowner in the parish in 1727 and it stands in front of Darley Farmhouse, the land of which supports sheep and cattle.

A mention of the tree in the *Western Morning News* in 1933 described it as 'growing steadily for the past two centuries', and it was then reported to bear 'a heavy crop of acorns'. Nowadays it produces few, if any, and has actually stopped growing, having presumably at last reached maturity.

Tables and chairs used to be put inside the hollow Darley Oak and tea and supper parties were held in it. It is possible that it was at one time also a 'dancing tree' in which people would dance, hence the 'pleasure parties' of the eighteenth century.

The present farmhouse was built in 1733 and the oak was already a curiosity then. With its venerable age the tree has, not unnaturally, collected several legends. It is said to have healing properties if one sits and meditates with one's back leaning against it, and an old superstition is that anyone who passed through it and then circled its girth would have all their wishes granted. Whether or not it was efficacious we do not know!

The tree is in a private garden and yard, so permission is needed to go close to it, although it can be partially seen from the public road which runs alongside the farm entrance.

55   LINKINHORNE

Daniel Gumb's 'House'

Linkinhorne was the parish in which was born in the eighteenth century a very remarkable man. Daniel Gumb grew up in a cottage on Bodmin Moor and from an early age showed signs of genius, not always recognised in those days. He read every book he could find, mastered the complexities of algebra and Euclid and wandered the moor, chipping rocks, while he dreamed about his obsession – the stars. He was given some tuition by William Cookworthy of Plymouth, the man who discovered how to use china clay to make porcelain, but Daniel yearned for the moor and the wandering way of life, so he earned his living as a stonemason, carving gravestones. When he decided to marry he also chose to build a stone house, so he combed the Caradon Hills for slabs of granite and slate moorstone. When he had accumulated enough of the right size and shape he built his house on the moor, not a great distance from what is now the village of Minions. It was a stone house to which he took his bride and they lived in harmony, sleeping on a bed of Cornish granite and with all stone furniture. The couple had several children and Daniel studied the stars and carved advanced geometrical diagrams on the

walls of his home. He died in 1776, a brilliant but unsung Cornishman, destined for great things but lacking the opportunity to achieve them.

Daniel Gumb's house no longer stands but remnants of it remain with geometric diagrams etched on some of the slate slabs which were once the walls of his home. These can be seen to this day if one is instructed where to look and are within walking distance of Minions, although the going is sometimes a bit rough.

THE LIZARD

The Rutways at Bessy's Cove

56

Around the coasts of Cornwall tales of smugglers and smuggling are never very far away and a 'tip off' about one unusual feature brought a variation on that theme.

The rutways at Bessy's Cove (once known as Smugglers' Cove) are surely unique. They are parallel grooves cut in some pretty grim-looking rocks on the foreshore which we are told were for the purpose of getting carts down to the beach at night to load ore into waiting ships; these in turn would unload the cargoes they had brought for the carts to take back inland.

At high tide the rocks are covered by the sea and the ruts allowed carts to be guided safely in the dark, almost as if they were trains on railway lines.

But another story that has survived the generations tells a slightly different tale. Locally it is believed that the channels were deliberately cut to

facilitate smuggling, with contraband goods being brought ashore under cover of darkness by carts which went down empty but came back fully loaded. The ruts are certainly a weird phenomenon and one can hardly believe it is true when told that they are natural fissures in the rocks.

In his book *A View from Trencom* Cornish author and publisher Bob Acton (who drew the picture above) gives some interesting information about them, saying that they are about 60yds long, about 16in deep and 4ft 4in apart. Surely nature would not have calculated two separate channels so accurately?

THE LIZARD

57

Serpentine

At one time it would have been unthinkable to return home from a holiday in Cornwall without a souvenir made of serpentine; it could be an ornament or a trinket, evocative of the rocks and beautiful scenery of the Lizard in the west of the county.

In their book *Serpentine* Michael Sagar-Fenton and Stuart B. Smith tell us that serpentine is not rare and 'The Lizard is not the only place in Britain that it occurs'. They go on to explain that it is found in France, Germany, Spain, Portugal and Canada, and a deposit 'in Australia [is] some four hundred miles in length'. But nowhere has serpentine been exploited to the extent that it has been on the Lizard, for many years.

The stone is so attractive; it ranges in colour and hue from green, yellow and red to brown and black. In addition to making souvenirs it was used as slabs of polished marble for worktops, and in Landewednack church-yard on the Lizard a number of the gravestones are of serpentine – it is a most versatile material.

In the nineteenth and early twentieth centuries several large quarries operated to provide the stone, and hundreds of craftsmen fashioned it into beautiful objects from trinkets such as brooches and earrings to church fonts and miniature versions of those, along with other objects to serve the tourist market. Most popular even today are miniature lighthouses, the base on which they stand being left as the unpolished rock. More elaborate lighthouses could be up to 2ft high or taller and these fine examples make a lot of money when sold today.

Sadly, the industry has now faded away to practically nothing, with only a handful of craftsmen still working the stone. It requires great skill to carve serpentine successfully, for the stone ranges from a very hard to an easily workable consistency and a craftsman needs to know his stone before starting work on it.

In Victorian days magnificent pieces, such as intricately fashioned vases, were made and very occasionally may be found in antiques shops today, with prices which reflect their rarity and the work and skill that has gone into making them.

Red serpentine was the most highly prized. But just a pebble from the beach or a piece of rough stone from the heathland above is a desirable souvenir.

LONDON APPRENTICE

58

The Horses' Drink

Everyone is familiar with horse troughs on the side of roads, although they have not been used much since the advent of the internal combustion engine, and Cornwall has something unique to serve this once very useful and necessary purpose.

By the side of the B3273 St Austell to Mevagissey road, approximately 400yds north of New Mills Primitive Methodist Chapel at London Apprentice is the Horses' Drink. It is set into a Cornish hedge forming part of Mulvra Farm. In an article in *Old Cornwall*, the journal of the Federation of Old Cornwall Societies, Mr David Stark of London Apprentice describes its construction:

Two sections of hedge were removed, possibly in the nineteen twenties, over a length of about six feet to give access from the highway to a small stream. The two ends of the hedge were faced with masonry over a length of about five feet and the tops of these were finished in mortar rendering. Livestock in the meadow through which the stream ran were prevented from straying on to the road by a four feet high iron fence. The three posts supporting the fence are lengths of former railway track.

The simple drinking facility is known locally, and has been for many, many years, as Horses' Drink and must have been the only place between St Austell and Pentewan where animals could drink.

Mr Stark cites the case of a former colleague who, as a lad, worked on a farm at St Ewe and took calves in a cart to market at St Austell, with the cow following unattached behind. The lad was always told, 'Mind you let the horses drink at Horses' Drink.'

This little feature remains exactly as it was built and is probably unique; there are no records of any similar construction in Cornwall. The Cornish always have shone in ingenuity and Cornwall has spawned many brilliant inventions!

LOOE

St George's Island (Looe Island)

This is perhaps a story you would find only in Cornwall, that land of surprises and eccentric people.

Many visitors stand on Hannafore Point at Looe and gaze across an often turbulent stretch of water to the little offshore St George's Island, known locally as Looe Island, and speculate about it, because from the mainland it can be seen that there is at least one sizeable house on the island.

The 22½-acre island is 1 mile around and 159ft high at its summit, but is like a little self-contained country, as anyone visiting it will appreciate.

The island was at one time a haven for smugglers and there was a Benedictine chapel, built in the eleventh century, on it; the only remains which can still be seen are two carved stones lying in the grass near the summit. The story is that the island was a safe hiding place for abbey treasures at the time of the Dissolution of the Monasteries in the sixteenth century, but that has never been proved.

The island has had a succession of owners over the years. In the eighteenth century a family called Finn lived there for many years; they were reputed to have exterminated the rabbit and rat populations by eating them.

In comparatively modern times the then owners cultivated a field for the growing of daffodils, which they sent to the mainland for onward transmission to London and other city markets hungry for early spring flowers.

In 1964 the island was bought by two remarkable spinsters, sisters Evelyn and Babs Atkins, who lived in suburban Surrey and followed the humdrum life of thousands of people who commuted daily to their work in London.

These two exceptional ladies lived for thirty-three years on their own paradise island just half a mile out to sea from East Looe. They welcomed visitors to the island and were supremely happy, working at several different crafts, the end products of which they sold to visitors. Evelyn also wrote two books about how they bought the island and their life on it. They lived a peaceful and fulfilled existence together with their beloved dogs and cats, until in 1997 Evelyn, the elder, died at the age of 87. Sister Babs lived on there alone until she too passed away a few years later. It was her greatest sadness that Caradon District Council would not allow her sister to be buried on the island, despite the fact that Evelyn had left instructions that she was to be buried there.

The council claimed that there was no suitable place on the island for a grave, no doubt envisaging 'luxury housing' springing up on it in the future, yet it was perfectly legal to be buried on private property so long as no nuisance was caused to neighbours, and the Atkins sisters were not going to cause a nuisance to anybody. But Evelyn was buried in West Looe cemetery. When Babs died the council relented and she is buried in the former daffodil field. It is a cause for regret to many people that the sisters, who had been inseparable for the whole of their long lives, could not rest together in death.

However, they had the last laugh because although developers had been greedily eyeing their island for many years (and the island which cost £22,000 in 1964 would probably be worth millions to developers), the sisters had turned down all offers for it. They bequeathed their island to the Cornwall Wildlife Trust, which now owns and manages the little paradise and ensures that it remains unspoilt.

The island is open to visitors during the summer and details of times and how to get there may be obtained on application to the Cornwall Wildlife Trust. It is well worth a visit.

LOSTWITHIEL

The Missing Word

In Lostwithiel churchyard there is a gravestone which commemorates a tragedy in the quiet country town. It has one very strange feature.

In 1814 England and the United States had been at war for four years and troop movements in Cornwall were commonplace. In August of that

year the 28th Regiment, having been succeeded at Pendennis Castle, Falmouth, by the 11th Regiment of Foot, was on a forced march to Plymouth and a halt was made at Lostwithiel. The men took advantage of the opportunity to indulge in drink and two of the soldiers became fighting drunk. Accompanied by two slightly more sober comrades, they demanded that the town constable provide a cart to convey them to the next halting place. However, the constable turned down the request, whereby the men threatened to shoot him.

The town serjeant, John Burnett, went to the scene of the disturbance and announced that he was going to take into custody the man who had fired a shot, one John Sims.

However, Sims was too drunk to see reason, shouting 'I'll shoot you first', and suiting action to words he discharged his musket at close range. The ball passed right through Burnett's body and he died within an hour on that fateful Sunday. Local bystanders turned furiously on Sims and he was taken into custody. He was executed on 31 March 1815 after being tried and sentenced at Launceston Assizes.

A beautifully carved gravestone stands above Burnett's grave but there is one curious thing about it. The inscription reads 'Joseph Burnett who was unfortunately shot by a Private of the 24th Regt. when in the execution of his as Peace Officer of this Borough on 21st August '14'. The curious thing is that the word 'duty' is omitted. Was the stone carver so overcome by the tragedy that he could not concentrate sufficiently on what he was doing and did not realise that he had left out a vital word? Or was there some other motive from the powers that be? The controversial thing is that no attempt was made later to add the missing word even though there was plenty of room for it without upsetting or cramping the rest of the inscription. There appears to be no valid reason for omitting that important word – or was there? We shall never know.

ST MABYN

61

The AA Sign

They were once a familiar sight in every village in England – the circular yellow and black enamel AA signs proclaiming the name of the village and giving details of mileage from London and neighbouring villages and hamlets.

They have long since disappeared from the rural scene and any that were saved are collectors' items. However, in St Mabyn they have preserved this distinctive relic of motoring days long past when traffic was sparse and satellite navigation systems were yet a distant invention. High up on a building in the centre of the village the St Mabyn AA sign is still in situ and no doubt passing motorists still find it useful.

MAKER

A Stone in a Stone!

62

A search around the older parts of Cornish churchyards often produces some unusual gravestones but none so peculiar as one in the churchyard just north of the tower of Maker church.

Little John Chubb was only 3 years 9 months old when he died in 1790 – a tragic end because it was caused by him swallowing a stone.

His distraught parents had a beautifully incised gravestone erected, and not content with a long and heart-rending epitaph they had a full-sized carving of the swallowed stone itself put on the gravestone alongside the second line of the inscription. The latter is very touching and perhaps one can detect a hint of bitterness, but whoever composed it was meticulous in recording the facts.

The epitaph reads as follows:

> Harsh were thy Cries and every piercing Groan
> Caus'd by the racking Torment of the Stone:
> Thy Hopeless State for Three revolving years:
> Each Night and Day call'd forth a Mother's Tears;
> Her tender Care and every Art was Vain
> To ease thy Woe or mitigate thy Pain:
> Till Heav'n in Pity bid such Torments cease
> And call'd thy Spirit to the Realms of Peace.

The rest of the inscription on the stone shows that the Chubbs were a tragic family, for it reveals that their son William died at the age of only two weeks and their second son, also William, died at the age of three weeks – a sad story indeed.

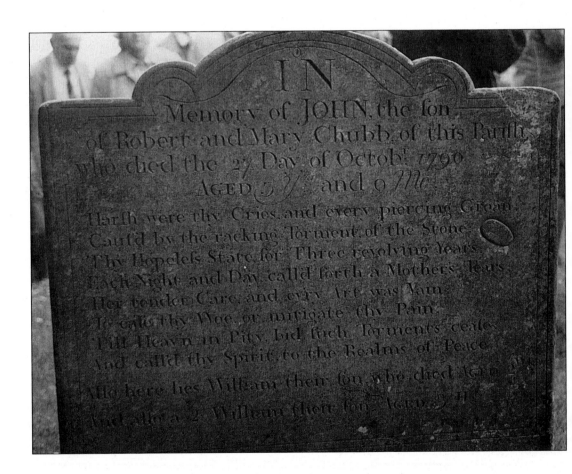

MANACCAN

Discovery of Titanium

63

Titanium is a substance which today plays a vital part in the manufacturing of a vast number of products ranging from plastics to hardened steel, face powder and other cosmetics, glassware, and even false teeth.

The dark grey metallic element found in small quantities in various minerals was first located in the watercourse of a Cornish mill. The Revd William Gregor, an amateur geologist and scientist, and rector of Creed from 1793 until his death in 1817, was the man who made the startling discovery, which in a way revolutionised many industries.

William Gregor sent for analysis a sample of a strange black magnetic sand which had been found in the watercourse of Manaccan and Tregonnell Mill. Puzzled by it, he began a series of experiments which proved to him that it had a metallic base. He continued his experiments and produced a slag which contained titanium. He called

his find 'Manaccanite' but it is now known as ilmenite, one of the main sources of titanium, but it was many years before its value was fully appreciated.

Titanium was named after the Titans of Greek mythology. Today deposits in Australia, Ceylon, Scandinavia and Canada are worked commercially on a large scale. The source of the black sand at Manaccan has long since disappeared but there is a tribute to Mr Gregor and his discovery in Manaccan church and samples of titanium are on display there in a special exhibit to honour the remote Cornish parish's great claim to fame.

64 MANACCAN AND ST NEWLYN EAST

The Fig Trees

Two arboreal marvels vie for notoriety in Cornwall and by remarkable coincidence they are both fig trees. They grow out of the masonry of church buildings and are very large and healthy but both appear to have no means of normal sustenance for big trees.

The Manaccan tree is known to have been growing for at least 200 years. The Norman walls of the tower from which it springs consist of two outer facings of stone with the intervening space filled with rubble, and it is from this rubble that the tree grows. Its size can best be seen in winter when the branches are bare, but it is a magnificent sight when in full leaf and expands year by year. It is, in fact, occasionally necessary to lop some branches on account of possible damage to the fabric of the building.

The St Newlyn East tree is slightly smaller and it grows out of the church porch. It, too, gets bigger and more vigorous as the years pass and shows no sign of wilting from lack of either soil or moisture.

Both trees have the same superstition attached to them, that if any of their branches are cut off, dire misfortune will befall the person responsible. At St Newlyn

East the tale is told by an elderly resident that the last brave man to lop some of the tree's branches had died soon afterwards. On enquiring the age of the unfortunate tree feller, expecting to hear of a tragedy of the death of a young man, it turned out that the wood cutter was actually ninety-two when he died. However, that superstition does not seem to take its toll in Manaccan, where the fig tree is regularly kept in check.

MARAZION

St Michael's Mount Tramway

65

The thousands of visitors to the National Trust's spectacular St Michael's Mount, on their way to start the climb up the path to the summit and the fine house and other buildings on the top of it, may notice a gap between cottages on the harbour and what appear to be railway lines going into it. If they are inquisitive enough to look more closely they may see the

entrance to a small tunnel, but most people do not see it as they are so anxious to reach the glories awaiting them at the top of the Mount.

What they are missing is the start of a unique tramway system. The Mount Tramway is the only such railway to be built in Cornwall. For over 100 years this miniature railway has been operational and is a vital part of living on the Mount. In its time it has covered over 20,000 miles travelling up and down the slope.

When the extension to the castle was completed in 1887 it was realised that a large establishment like a stately home has to be serviced with provisions, fuel, building materials and so on, and passage by horse and cart up the steep, narrow and stony path to the summit was not adequate. So was born the 200yds tramway, which because of the nature of the unusual route had to be built through a tunnel along almost its whole length, with a gradient of 1 in 3½, even 1 in 2 at its steepest point.

The tracks are 2ft 5½in-gauge and the tunnel is 5ft wide and 7ft high; the little wagons are worked by cable, with the winding gear and other machinery housed in the building beside the harbour entrance to the tunnel.

During its life the tramway has been powered by three different systems – at first belt driven off a gas engine, then an electric motor, and now by mains electricity after an 11,000-volt power cable was brought across from the mainland to the Mount.

The tramway normally takes four or five runs daily and every imaginable type of commodity is carried on it. Lord St Leven's Coronation regalia was even transported via the tramway.

Although the tramway is not open to the public, it is possible to peer into the yard and see the tunnel entrance, and perhaps a wagon on the rails, as one passes on the public highway.

ST MARTIN-BY-LOOE

66

Coloured Bench Ends

Cornwall is well known for its interesting collection of bench ends in churches throughout the county, but only one church can claim something entirely different. In the south aisle of St Martin-by-Looe church is the only coloured bench end in Cornwall, possibly in the country.

It was put in the church in memory of a British army officer drowned in India in the days of the Raj. It is divided into four delightfully carved little pictures, one showing the oasis of Hunh, the second a man sitting outside a mountain hut in north Kashmir (presumably the deceased when on an expedition into the mountains) and the third and fourth with views of the River Indus and the Himalayan mountains. The painting is delicate and restrained and the pictures very realistic.

As artefacts that show the artistic rather than the historical side of life, the bench ends can hardly be bettered. All the bench ends in the church (with the exception of the War Memorial pew and the coloured ones), were carved between 1923 and 1948 by a very remarkable and talented Plymouth lady, Miss Violet Pinwill, whose work appears in many churches in Cornwall and Devon. Miss Pinwill was regarded as a 'one off' as not many young ladies went in for wood carving at that time, it being considered a not very ladylike pursuit.

ST MAWGAN-IN-PYDAR

67

The Hodbarrow Miner

There was always a close link between Cornwall and the northern county of Cumbria. In the mighty Hodbarrow Iron Mine on the then Cumberland shore of the Dudden estuary, which operated between 1855 and 1968, pumps were installed from Harvey and Co. of Hayle and from the Perran Foundry in Cornwall, and Cornishman Sir John Coode had been the mine's first resident engineer. The Hodbarrow company had its own fleet of ships, which delivered coal and pit wood to the mine and carried away iron ore to far distant locations as well as transporting other cargoes.

On 6 March 1908 one of the ships in this fleet, a schooner named *Hodbarrow Miner*, was en route from Runcorn, Cheshire, to Truro with coal, when in heavy seas and a strong gale from west-north-west the ship beached and then capsized off Mawgan Porth when the crew abandoned ship. According to Richard Gillis in his book *A Sea Miscellany of Cornwall and the Isles of Scilly* the master, Richard Tyrran, who had been her skipper for fourteen years, was knocked overboard and drowned when jibbing the vessel 20 miles off the Longships. The rest of the crew tried to carry on for shelter.

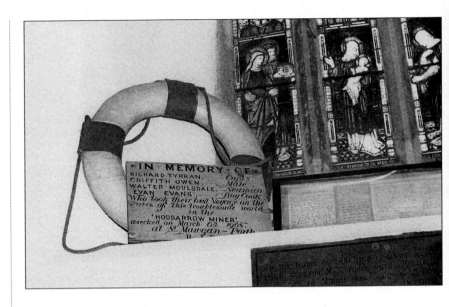

After the capsize one of the crew was rescued by a coastguard who waded into the heavy surf to save him but the remaining crew members perished. One body, that of Griffith Owen, the mate, was washed ashore and buried in the churchyard of St Mawgan-in-Pydar. He was only 25 years of age. His family later erected a rather fine gravestone above his last resting place, the inscription including a passage from the Bible in Welsh and a carved decoration on the stone of two anchors.

At the time of the tragedy the rector of St Mawgan wrote to the vicar of Amlwch Port, Anglesey – the parish from which the crew came – informing him that the parishioners of St Mawgan would be arranging a simple memorial to the four men. In reply he received a grateful letter from the Revd T. Prichard at Amlwch, containing the information that seaman Walter Mousdale and the boy cook Evan Evans had been members of his Sunday school and adding that Evans had been a newspaper boy in the town until he joined the ship in which he lost his life, it being his first voyage.

In St Mawgan church the members of the congregation placed a memorial board as well as the framed letters from Mr Prichard and others and a photograph of the beached ship before she capsized. Also included in the memorial display was a lifebelt (presumably from the *Hodbarrow Miner*). It can be a very moving experience to view these relics, which bring home, so poignantly, awareness of the cruelty of the Cornish seas.

In recent years the church has been refurbished but the *Hodbarrow Miner* relics remain on view, apart from the letters which have been removed for safe keeping as sunlight was fading the writing.

Griffith Owen's grave can be seen in the churchyard. The mainmast of the *Hodbarrow Miner* became the flagstaff of Glendorgal, then the country house of the Tangye family, but whether or not it is still there is not known.

ST MAWGAN IN PYDAR

The Hope Tragedy

68

The inhabitants of this parish in north Cornwall have a constant reminder in their church and churchyard of the perils of the spectacular but cruel rocks around their stretch of coastline and the ferocity of the seas as they pound those rocks. The memorials to the shipwrecks of the *Hodbarrow Miner* and the *Hope*, which were both appalling tragedies, are ever present reminders of the dangers.

On 12 December 1846 a longboat drifted silently into Mawgan Porth. It had come from the Liverpool barque *Hope*, homeward bound from Rio de Janeiro with a cargo of guano. This ship had been badly damaged off the Irish coast but had somehow managed to sail on until final abandonment was forced off Fishguard Bay. Ten men, including Captain Jones, in a longboat, were spotted by a schooner, but a blinding snowstorm made rescue difficult and the longboat drifted away. The crew of the schooner, thinking it empty, allowed it to go. But the longboat held a gruesome secret and it was then too late to do anything about it.

The men in the bottom of the longboat, without food and water, soon succumbed to the near arctic conditions, and when the boat finally grounded off Mawgan Porth the ten crew members in it had all frozen to death.

The stern of the longboat was inscribed as a memorial to the ten who died; they included the cabin boy, known only as 'Jemmy'. When the wooden stern deteriorated a replica was produced and it today marks the grave in St Mawgan churchyard of those ten brave souls. It is a poignant reminder of the cruelty of waves and weather. After the list of names, the inscription on the board says, 'who were drifted ashore in a boat, frozen to death, at Tregurrian Beach in this parish on Sunday 13th Dec. MDCCCXLVI'.

There is an interesting footnote to this story. In 1808 Cornish MP John Hearle Tremayne introduced the Dead Bodies Interment Bill in Parliament, which resulted in a ruling that there must be Christian burial for all victims of shipwreck, with expenses paid by the county and a reward for those discovering a body. The men from the barque *Hope* were the first to be buried in St Mawgan churchyard in accordance with the new law.

69

MINSTER

The Scissors

The little church of St Merthiana at Minster, near the village of Boscastle, is situated in a deep, wooded valley and is reached by a steep path from the road, beneath which it nestles. It is an idyllic setting in spring and summertime, but in the winter, when the wind howls through

the trees and the rain lashes down, it can be quite eerie and one almost expects to see the ghost of Welsh princess Madryn (to whom the church is dedicated as St Merthiana) to materialise out of the mist. She died in the sixth century and is said to be buried in the chancel area of the church.

The church has one curiosity – a carving of a pair of scissors on the outside of the tower. Despite all efforts to discover the origin and meaning of this strange symbol it has proved impossible to find out anything. They could date from the sixteenth century.

The church suffered very badly from the disastrous floods in Boscastle in August 2004, when a deluge of water roared down the Valency valley after sudden torrential rainfall.

70

MORVAH

The Church of St Briget of Sweden

Apart from the Cornish, Celtic and Irish saints to whom churches in Cornwall are dedicated, at Morvah in west Cornwall, not far from Land's End, there is something quite different and unique. The church there is the Church of St Briget of Sweden, the only church in Britain dedicated to this Swedish saint.

A 'new' church was erected at Morvah in the latter part of the fourteenth century, on the site of the present building, and reputedly the Knights of St John were responsible, while an episcopal document dated 7 May 1390 refers to a Chapelry of St Briget in the parish of Madron, since identified with Morvah church. From the church leaflet we learn that the name 'Sancta Brigida' in the document is believed to refer to St Briget (variously Brigid or Birgitta) of Sweden, whose cult was extremely popular in Britain at that time and who was called a saint by

the locals even before her delayed canonisation on 8 October 1391. The church of St Briget at Morvah was formally licensed for divine services by the Bishop of Exeter on 22 September 1400.

The Swedish community in Britain takes a special interest in Morvah church and among its treasures are candlesticks and communion cruets of Swedish glass, given as gifts, a Swedish national flag presented by the Rotary Club of Vadstena (the place in Sweden associated with St Briget), and a magnificent glass 'iceberg' on which is beautifully engraved the outline of the church. The latter was a gift from Mr Eskil Vilhelmsson, when he was manager of the Torrington Glassworks in north Devon.

The church leaflet is printed in both English and Swedish and of course the church receives many Swedish visitors. The Swedish version of the leaflet contains rather more information about St Briget herself than the English version.

71 MORWENSTOW

'Church Towers' chimneys

The eccentric vicar of Morwenstow, the Revd Robert Stephen Hawker (1803–75), built his own vicarage, as the previous one was in a ruinous state when he arrived. He decided that a heavy Victorian-Gothic edifice was suited to his position in the parish and he wanted only views of the church and the sea from his windows, so the house was angled in such a way that the windows embrace those two features. He based the building on a model in T.F. Hunt's *Designs for Parsonage Houses.* Unusual as the building is, the most curious feature is the chimneys. These Hawker had built as replicas of towers of the churches in the places where he had lived and served – Stratton, North Tamerton, Whitstone and Oxford – while the kitchen chimney was styled in the form of his mother's tomb.

Another unusual feature of the vicarage is a slate tablet above the front door on which is incised a verse which Hawker himself wrote:

> A House, a Glebe, a Pound a Day,
> A Pleasant Place to Watch and Pray.
> Be true to Church be kind to Poor,
> O Minister, for ever more.

The tablet is carefully preserved in situ by the present owners of the house and is a vivid reminder of the builder and first occupant.

MORWENSTOW

Hawker's hut

Memories of 'Passon' Hawker, as he was known locally, abound in Morwenstow and the National Trust owns a tangible reminder of this remarkable man. Robert Hawker built a little shanty under the towering cliffs, constructed entirely of driftwood which he collected from beneath the

cliffs, hauling it up from the almost inaccessible small beach below, much of it probably being the remains of ships wrecked on the treacherous rocks.

In this little building Hawker retreated to write his poems and songs and to meditate. He often sat for hours in it, obsessed with the idea that a storm was brewing and that shipwreck would ensue, requiring his assistance and priestly administrations. He was famous for rescuing and helping shipwrecked sailors and bringing the bodies of those who had perished into the churchyard for burial, for he was the most compassionate of men.

His hut is now the National Trust's smallest property and it is possible to walk to it. It is believed by some people that it is haunted by Robert Hawker and it certainly has a strangely mystical atmosphere, especially on a stormy day.

ST NEOT

73

Carnglaze Slate Caverns

The true slates, orkyllas, of Cornwall have been mined for hundreds of years and slate quarries, like the famous Delabole Quarries, are normally huge open-cast pits. But Carnglaze slate caverns are unique in the county because there the slate was mined from underground chambers. The quarrying cut into the hillside and it was found that by driving under the hill better-quality slate could be obtained.

The actual size of these extraordinary caverns may never be known. Even the full extent of them will forever remain a mystery. With the exception of dividing pillars of rock between the chambers, the roofs, even with their tremendous extent, are totally unsupported, demonstrating the remarkable strength and stability of these particular beds of slate.

During the Second World War the caverns played an important part. They were used as a major depot for the safe storage of vast quantities of rum for the Royal Navy.

After mining operations ceased the caverns remained empty and silent until 1973 when members of the public were admitted to visit them for the first time. The going was a bit rough but visitors were astounded when they first glimpsed the huge upper chamber, approximately 300ft long and 40 to 50ft wide, as well as being up to 20ft in height. A long flight of steps leads down to the floor of the caverns and here another breathtaking sight awaits – after a short walk an underground lake is reached. Its appearance is quite stunning: it has been compared to the famous Blue Grotto in Capri. The water is over 30ft deep and is totally clear but a beautiful bluish-green colour.

Nowadays the access to the caverns is very much improved and the glorious first cavern has been converted into an auditorium, with seating for 400 people, where musical and theatrical performances take place.

The caverns are open all year and truly are a Cornish curiosity.

ST NEOT

74

King Charles II Commemoration Branch

Visitors to St Neot may be surprised to see what appears to be a small tree or branch of a tree sprouting out of the top of the church tower. They should not jump to the conclusion that it is untidy to allow vegetation to grow out of the masonry.

This must surely be one of the most curious symbols of commemoration in Britain. At the time of King Charles II, when the Civil War raged around the village, a Royalist stronghold, a local benefactor of the time left a small sum of money with a very strange condition attached to the bequest – that a branch of an oak tree, with an oak apple on it, be fixed on the top of the fourteenth-century tower of St Neot church every 29 May to commemorate the famous time when Charles II hid in an oak tree after the Battle of Worcester, before being later restored to the throne. The stipulation was that even when the branch withered it was still to be left in place on the tower until replaced by a fresh branch on the following 29 May.

This custom has been faithfully carried out without fail over the years and to this day the branch remains in its lofty situation on the tower for all to see and (one hopes) remember King Charles II.

75

ST NEWLYN EAST

Hinkypunks

Hinkypunks were common to both Cornwall and Devon and in medieval times were a force with which to be reckoned. These legendary mythological beings were believed to be spirits that were the original inhabitants of Bodmin Moor and Dartmoor. They came in two varieties, good and bad, but the bad ones outweighed the good. The sole purpose of the bad ones was to lure unwary travellers into deadly bogs on the moors; they would stand

by laughing as the unfortunate people got sucked into the mire. The good hinkypunks led travellers away from the bogs, thus ensuring safe passage.

The hinkypunks provided subjects for some medieval carvers of church bench ends. Since no one had ever seen a hinkypunk nobody could say what they looked like, although they were believed to have one leg and one arm. So medieval carvers could let their imagination run riot and depict the hinkypunks as they thought they must look. There is one example of a hinkypunk on a bench end in St Newlyn East church. It is a rarity in Cornwall, not always recognised for what it is.

NEWQUAY

Burton's Stile

Stiles are an intrinsic part of Cornish life. They come in many varieties – granite, slate, wood, iron – whatever local material is suitable for the purpose or comes to hand, but none is more strange than Burton's Stile on a footpath between St Columb Minor and Porth. It is a very sturdy affair of stone, incised on one side 'Burton's Stile 1857' and on the other with carved images of a bottle, a glass and a flagon and the words 'The Fall of Man 1857'.

It commemorates a man called Burton, a pedlar who toured the villages around the area, and also quite frequently the not-far-distant Cornish Arms. He traded in earthen-ware vessels – jars, pots, pitchers, etc. – which he carried in a pack on his head. One day in 1857 he was so inebriated as he trod the footpath with his rather cumbersome load that that he fell at this spot and was lucky to survive.

His close encounter with eternity changed his life for ever. When he sobered up he realised his dangerous and foolish habit and treated drink with respect for the rest of his life. As a result of this he pulled his life together and in due course became a successful businessman. As a warning to all who may be tempted to head for a downfall in the way that he did, he erected this stile, which presumably replaced a much more primitive one. It is probably the only inscribed stile in Cornwall.

NEWQUAY

The Huer's Hut

It sounds picturesque and quite romantic but ask most people what a 'huer' is and they will probably not be able to give an answer.

Huge shoals of pilchards were caught off the Cornish coast in the nineteenth century. According to Keith Harris in his book *Hevva!*, one such shoal enclosed and landed at St Ives in 1851 was estimated to have contained 16,500,005 fish, weighing in at 1,100 tons. The huer was a very important person in the great days of pilchard fishing. Keith Harris tells us that in the summer months great shoals of pilchards would appear as a stain of red, purple or silver in the water 'while overhead flocks of screaming gulls and plummeting gannets marked their position from the air'.

As the shoals came in, the granite buttresses of Land's End split the shoals into two separate ones, and the northern shoal would carry on right up the north Cornish coast.

Nicholas Ashton, in his book *Among Cornish Fisher Folk*, published in 1894, explains how the huer was an experienced man stationed in a lookout onshore. He would call 'Hevva' through a long tin trumpet to alert the fishermen that the shoals were in sight. He then had the vitally important task of directing the shooting and recovery of the seine net, and this he did by using a complicated set of semaphore signals.

If a huer made a mistake or gave the wrong signals it could spell disaster for the pilchard seine fishermen, so his job was a tremendously weighty one and his thorough knowledge of it was vital.

When the great shoals deserted Cornwall and the pilchard fishing industry died the huer's hut at Newquay was retained, and it stands to this day as a memorial to the very brave men who underwent untold hardship, not to mention the anguish of their families as the men toiled to harvest 'the little silver darlings'. The huer's hut is constructed of rubble, is whitewashed so that it would be conspicuous to the fishing boats, has an outside staircase leading to its one floor and is as sturdy as it was when the huer made his calls from it.

NORTH CORNWALL

78

'Little Trees'

On a few beaches in north Cornwall it is possible occasionally to find the exquisite and locally prized 'little trees', as they are called. These are actually

the skeletons of a deep sea coral, known as fan coral, which, when alive, is bright pink in colour. They are washed ashore when they die, having been dislodged from the rocks on the seabed to which they cling. The wiry, dark brown stems look like daintily branched polished mahogany.

A local belief is that they are lucky and that a home will never burn down if it has a 'little tree' in it.

The distribution on the beaches is very localised, reflecting where the colonies of coral thrive far out at sea, and 'trees' are most likely to be found after winter storms have triggered very heavy seas. The best place to locate them is along the tide line where they become tangled with debris washed up on the beach by the sea.

PADSTOW

79

Civil War 'Deception'

In Prideaux Place, Padstow, the beautiful and historic home of Mr and Mrs Peter Prideaux-Brune and their family, is a curiosity which is unique and should not be missed. Among the display of miniatures in the drawing room is a bizarre relic of the Civil War. It is a rather unflattering portrait of King Charles I but it holds a secret. On the reverse is a likeness of Oliver Cromwell.

The Prideaux family at that time supported the Parliamentary cause in the Civil War but were related to the famous seafaring family of Grenville who lived at nearby Stowe and who were strong Royalists. So at Prideaux Place dinner guests were carefully chosen and the miniature, which could be worn as a pendant on a chain, would be worn facing outwards according to the allegiance of the guests.

The Prideaux family have been at Prideaux Place ever since Sir Nicholas Prideaux built the earliest part of it in the sixteenth century, since when fourteen generations have lived there. The house is open to the public and this tiny gem should be looked out for when visiting the house.

80

PADSTOW

The Little Horseman

In Padstow's busy streets there is little chance to stand and stare, but it is well worth braving the traffic to look up to the roof of a building which now houses a bank in the centre of the town. There high up on the ridge of the roof is the Little Horseman. He is not the most elegant of horsemen and his mount may even be mistaken for a lion but he is an important part of south-west history. He is actually a terracotta ridge tile; originally there were two horsemen on the building but unfortunately only one remains today.

They featured on a picture postcard in the early 1920s which carried an inscription saying that the premises supplied horsemen as King's Messengers. That is a theory but the Little Horseman is truly an enigma; no one really knows what he signified. The most popular explanation is that the horsemen denoted that the house owner was a Royalist who offered shelter to fellow Royalists in the turbulent times of the Civil War. Another idea is that the figures were put on houses which had sheltered Prince Charles, who had ordered them to be erected. Then again some say they marked post stages in the time of stage coach travel, but that is also pure conjecture.

Terracotta is not the most durable of materials exposed to the elements and several Cornish examples have disappeared over the years, including one in Polperro and one in St Ives. There were two quite elegant examples in Devon, one in Exeter, the other in Ashburton, but the Exeter one was lost in the blitz in the Second World War.

As far as is known no examples have been recorded outside Cornwall and Devon, so the Padstow horseman is a pearl without price in its field.

PENZANCE

The Egyptian House

81

There are several examples of strange architecture in Cornwall but none more so than the Egyptian House in Penzance. Incongruous, maybe; unusual, most certainly!

In 1834 Penzance bookseller John Lavin bought two cottages in Chapel Street for £396 and proceeded to raise the height of the building and to add to its street front the present remarkable pseudo-Egyptian façade. The royal arms on the building suggest that it was complete before the accession of Queen Victoria in June 1837.

John Lavin's main business was in minerals, which he bought, sold and exhibited in his 'new' building. He also sold maps, guides and stationery in the Egyptian House. It is believed the exotic building must have been intended to emphasise the bizarre and beautiful side of geological specimens and also to attract visitors to his shop. At the time there was a great deal of interest in the study of minerals and fossils, particularly in Cornwall.

Many of the rare specimens sold by John Lavin were found by Cornish miners during the course of their work underground and others were conveyed to him by those who had worked in mining overseas and brought him back specimens when they came home. Mr Lavin is supposed to have been guilty of the occasional deception, but as an astute businessman he probably saw no harm in that.

Of John Lavin's two sons, the elder, Edward, ran a stationery, bookbinding and printing business in the Egyptian House beside the minerals shop, renting the premises from his father. However, in 1863, a few years after his father's death, he sold the entire collection of minerals for the sum of £2,500 to the Victorian philanthropist Angela Georgiana, Baroness Burdett-Coutts, and with the proceeds he built a large hotel on the Esplanade at Penzance, calling it Lavin's Hotel. It is now the Mount's Bay House Hotel.

After the French occupation of Egypt from 1789 to 1831 the Egyptian style appealed to those seeking novelty and publicity and the Egyptian House would seem to be one such example.

It has never been proved which architect was responsible for the design of the Egyptian House. Several famous architects of the day have had their names linked with it, but there is no evidence to connect any of them to the Egyptian House.

The Lavin family owned the house until 1910, after which it had several different owners until bought in 1968 by the Landmark Trust, a charity which specialises in the restoration of buildings of architectural and historic importance and finds a modern use for them which does not in any way detract from their character or historical significance. A great deal of work had to be done to the building to conserve it and it now houses three charming flats, each running the whole width of the building, with two shops beneath.

It was found that much of the ornamentation on the front of the building was made of Coade stone, the popular artificial stone manufactured at Lambeth in London and used for a variety of purposes, including gravestones.

Nothing has changed in the original appearance of the façade; even the royal arms were repainted, and what you see now is the same sight that passers-by saw when they admired John Lavin's showcase front to his building in the nineteenth century.

PENZANCE

The Gingko Tree

82

There are probably not more than two or three Gingko trees in Cornwall but one of them is rather special. The Gingko Biloba is a Japanese tree with handsome fan-shaped leaves. It is also sometimes known as the Maidenhair tree. The Gingko is regarded as a living fossil because specimens of its leaves have been found in fossils millions of years old and they do not differ from the leaves and structure of today's Gingkos.

Examples are usually found in large and very long-established gardens where they have plenty of room to spread themselves (there is, for instance, a large and quite famous specimen in Kew Gardens in London). The Penzance tree is successful against all the odds. For one thing it is flourishing in the corner of a town centre car park, almost abutting a busy main road, with all the pollution from traffic fumes and, one would imagine, very little soil to nurture its roots.

The Gingko has been in its somewhat inhospitable location for as long as anyone can remember, but its leaves are strong and shiny, and it spreads itself rather more upwards than outwards and is an attractive shape. It could at one time have been in a more natural environment in the nearby Morrab Gardens before the roads and car park were constructed, because these gardens were once the private grounds of a fine mansion, now housing the Morrab Library. Another Gingko tree can be seen almost opposite St George's Hall in Penzance.

PORTHCURNOW

83

The Logan Stone

The Logan Stone is a natural curiosity, a huge block of granite estimated to weigh somewhere in the region of 60 tons. It is so delicately poised upon a pile of other rocks that just a slight push can send it rocking, but it never falls.

For thousands of years the Logan Stone would rock at just the touch of a fingertip until the year 1824 when along came a mischievous young blade, a naval officer by the name of Lieutenant Goldsmith, a nephew of

the famous dramatist Oliver Goldsmith and at the time in command of a cutter. He had many times seen the Logan Stone while scanning the coast for smugglers as part of his naval duties and had seen people setting it rocking. On this fateful occasion he decided he would do something which he thought clever; he landed a boat crew and with the use of a marline spike and the aid of his brawny sailors he dislodged the stone and sent it crashing down on to the rocks below.

But he paid dearly for his prank. There was public outcry about the desecration of a Cornish landmark and the Admiralty ordered him to replace it exactly as it was before and at his own expense.

The cost of the operation was £124 10*s* 6*d* a lot of money for a young naval officer in those days, and there were rumours that the expense ruined Goldsmith. It apparently took several months and a great deal of hard manual work to get the stone back into its original position and, most important of all, to have it rocking again, as before.

The attempt was successful but the Logan Stone is now protected from meddlesome hands. It is visited by thousands of visitors every year who can only look and admire but cannot test its remarkable properties.

PORTHPEAN

84

The Boer War Memorial

Memorials commemorating the Boer Wars of the late nineteenth and early twentieth centuries are not very common and in Cornwall there is one unlike any other in the country.

In years gone by the village of Porthpean had no mains water supply and villagers had to rely on the village pump for their water. In many cases these indispensable objects were removed when they became redundant in later years but the one at Porthpean, near St Austell, was put to good use – it was transformed into a war memorial.

The pump is still there and attached to it is the original metal plaque, which is inscribed 'To Commemorate PEACE 1902. Given by Rose, Lady Graves-Sawle'. This unique memorial pays homage to many brave Cornishmen who fought in the campaign to which this memorial refers – the second Boer War of 1899–1902. The first war between the British and the Boers (Dutch settlers) of the Transvaal, South Africa, was caused when the Transvaal was declared a republic. Peace was made shortly afterwards, the British recognising the independence of the Transvaal. But a second war, with Britain on one side and the Transvaal Republic and the Orange Free State on the other, broke out in 1899, peace being signed on 31 May 1902. Many Cornishmen fought in the famous battles of that war such as Ladysmith and Mafeking.

85

PORT QUIN

A Rich Man's Pleasure

Little Doyden Castle nestles under the shelter of rising ground on the windswept Doyden Point on the north Cornish coast. The small crenellated building with spectacular views out to sea is a bit pretentious

in calling itself a castle, but a castle it was to its owner. The National Trust, which now owns the property, tells us that it was built in the 1820s by Captain Connor, a former prison governor, as a retreat where he and his friends could party to their heart's content without interference. Doyden Castle probably saw wild parties and gambling sessions, and was a safe haven to which to take favourite lady friends.

The little two-storey tower has a shallow one-storey extension, also crenellated, and it is let by the National Trust as holiday accommodation in the holiday season.

Doyden Castle achieved certain notoriety in the television series based on the *Poldark* novels, when it was home to one of the characters in the story, Dwight Enys.

86

POUNDSTOCK

The Gildhouse

Poundstock Gildhouse – its original spelling corrupted over the years – is a very rare north Cornwall building, considered to be the finest of its type in Cornwall.

The Gildhouse was built in the fifteenth century. It was beautifully constructed by local craftsmen using the local materials of the day – cob, local stone and slate – and is sited close to the ancient church dedicated to St Winwaloe. It was originally built as a meeting place for the parish guilds, a sort of combination of friendly society, social club and religious fraternities who oversaw the well-being of the parish. It was a hub of parish life and all activities revolved around it.

In the seventeenth century the Gildhouse served as a poorhouse and even a schoolroom. Over the years it fell into decline structurally and although still used on occasions its importance as a meeting place also

declined. The Gildhouse is a Grade I listed building and well worthy of restoration. In 2005 salvation appeared to be at hand. A Heritage Lottery Fund planning grant was obtained and it is hoped the building can be restored to tip-top condition. It can be visited by application to the church.

REDRUTH

The Insulting Gargoyles

87

You may need binoculars to be able to fully appreciate this curiosity. Look high up on the eastern side of the Norman tower of Redruth church to see two gargoyles depicting King Henry VII and his queen, Elizabeth of York. They are definitely not flattering depictions. Legend has it that they were an angry response to the slaughter by the King's men of the Cornish rebels led by Thomas Flamank of Bodmin and Michael Joseph (An Gof) of St Keverne, after they marched to London and were mown down by the King's forces at Blackheath in 1497. Among the carvings of angels and fanciful grotesques they are quite prominent. Experts claim that their authenticity can be gauged as the headgear on the male gargoyle is similar to that worn by King Henry in portraits of him.

88

ROCHE

Roche Rock

A 100ft-high rock with a chapel perched on top of it is surely one curiosity only Cornwall would claim. Roche Rock is there for all to see, and one cannot imagine what possessed our ancestors in the fifteenth century to build a chapel dedicated to St Michael, incorporating a hermit's cell, in such a difficult to reach position.

The rock itself is a giant outcrop composed of a very hard type of granite known in Cornwall as schorl, which contains the mineral tourmaline in its composition. Arthur Mee in his book *Cornwall*, in the King's England series, tells us that for two years the chapel was used for worship while the local church was being restored over 500 years

ago. We can only observe that the members of the congregation must have been a very athletic lot in those days!

Arthur Mee also quotes a sixteenth-century Cornish historian who wrote of Roche Rock: 'In this rugged pile may be observed several works: The first of Nature, the next of Force, the third of Art, which raised a building upon so craggy a foundation, the fourth of Industry, lastly of Devotion, and to this may be added a sixth work, even of Time.'

Nowadays a vertical iron ladder makes both ruined chapel and cell accessible to the adventurous and sure-footed. Views from the top are spectacular, but only for those with a head for heights.

ST THOMAS'S, RIVERSIDE

The Prior's Trumpet Boy

An unusual carving in stone on the left of the entrance porch of historic St Thomas's Church at Riverside, Launceston, has always been known as the Prior's Trumpet Boy and there is a good reason for that. The one-time Augustinian priory adjacent to the church gave its prior's name to the packhorse bridge across the River Kensey and to the Trumpet Boy.

A booklet compiled by the late Otho Peter in 1900 explains that a trumpeter was the forerunner of today's town crier. An entry in the accounts for Dunheved (Launceston) in 1493 refers to 3*s* 4*d* being paid to a trumpeter of the lord prior of Launceston to announce a death. The carving has suffered the ravages of time but is still quite recognisable.

SALTASH

Mary Newman's Cottage

Mary Newman's Cottage is a misnomer if ever there was one, but it saved this historic and interesting building from demolition. For more years than most people care to remember, 48 Culver Road, Saltash, has been referred to as 'Mary Newman's Cottage'.

Mary Newman was the first wife of Sir Francis Drake and there is an old tradition that she lived in the cottage before her marriage. However, Mary lived in St Budeaux, Plymouth, and was married in the parish church there in 1569; after her death in Plymouth in 1583 she was buried at St Budeaux.

Mary is first linked to Saltash in a story published in a monthly penny magazine in 1865. Colin Squires of Saltash Heritage has done a great deal of research into the subject and it is thanks to him that we know the story of this famous cottage. He has proved that the author of the story set it in what is today 48 Culver Road.

Quite apart from the Newman–Drake legend which draws hundreds of people from all over the world to visit it, the house is the oldest Tudor building in Saltash. It stands on one of the burgage plots laid out when the Borough of Saltash was founded in the twelfth century and the present structure dates from about 1500. In its prime it would have been one of the best dwellings in Saltash, probably beginning life as a merchant's house. It is rated as a rare and important survival.

It is fortunate that the Mary Newman legend existed, because it ensured that the house was excluded from the town's Waterside redevelopment scheme that commenced in 1957, when there was not the keen appreciation there is today of history and the need for preservation and conservation.

The cottage is now leased to the Tamar Protection Society by Caradon District Council and the society has done a splendid job in restoring the house and laying out the garden. The furniture in the house is on loan from the Victoria and Albert Museum, London, and other sources provide a wonderfully authentic atmosphere to the interior. A recent Heritage Lottery Fund grant will enable the garden to be recreated as an authentic Elizabethan garden and a further substantial grant from Cornwall Environment Trust will enable much conservation work to be done on the cottage. The Tamar Protection Society opens it to the public at certain times.

SALTASH

The Tillie Effigy

One of the most curious examples of Cornish eccentricity is on the Pentillie estate which contains a hill known as Mount Ararat. There stands a very surprising and 'creepy' monument to an extraordinary man.

Sir James Tillie was born of humble parentage but he was fortunate in marrying the daughter of Sir Harry Vane, and somehow by false pretences he claimed a knighthood. Finally his deception was uncovered by the College of Heralds, which revoked his grant of arms and fined him £100. Undeterred, he continued to call himself 'Sir' and through the years has always been remembered locally by that title.

Tillie died in 1712 and left explicit instructions that he was to be placed in the folly tower, which was intended as his mausoleum, dressed in his best clothes, seated on a chair and with books, pen and ink on a desk in front of him, to await the Day of Judgement. His wish was granted, but only partially. It was a leaden effigy of him that was placed in the tower and there it remains to this day, frighteningly lifelike and still visible if one is prepared to fight one's way through the vegetation to reach the tower.

The tower is now almost eclipsed by ivy and in a somewhat ruinous state. The square tower was a three-storeyed structure and is surrounded by a wall. A flight of ten steps leads up to the now-blocked entrance porch and in a stone grill set in the doorway is a peephole through which it is possible to peer to observe the effigy. The latter is now covered in ferns and brambles which will eventually envelop it altogether, but it is unbelievably eerie to look through the grill and see the lifelike seated figure, hands on thighs, waiting patiently. It is a curiosity really deserving of preservation.

Up to less than a hundred years ago local people really believed that it was actually Tillie sitting there and there are people who, within living memory, would not have gone near the place.

92

SALTASH

Two Gravestones

Most people have one memorial stone erected above their grave, but in a chapel cemetery in Saltash one man has had two stones erected in his name. Joseph Rawling, who died on 30 March 1886, was married twice and most unusually both his wives erected their own stones above his grave. One might think that happened in very ancient times but these stones are comparatively modern.

SALTASH

The 'Union Flag' Building

93

Cornwall has many fine and unusual buildings but surely none more bizarre or eccentric than the Union Inn at Saltash, the front of which is painted as a giant Union flag. The flag is formed of the red cross of St George (England), and the white and red diagonal crosses of St Andrew (Scotland) and St Patrick (Ireland) on a blue ground.

The painting of the inn was originally intended as a temporary measure to commemorate the fiftieth anniversary of VE Day in 1995, but it proved such an eye-catcher that it has been retained and is now a distinctive landmark for all travellers by train over Brunel's Royal Albert Bridge and by road over the Tamar Road Bridge. The building also has colourful murals skilfully painted on its gable end by local artist David Wheatley.

94

SANCREED

Fougous

Fougous are a bit of a mystery because no one knows what their real purpose was, so we can only speculate. They are long, low underground passages, cleverly walled and roofed with large stones which have stood the test of time for thousands of years, and because they are usually located near the sites of former dwellings they are believed to have been used for storage, probably of food.

A fougou near Carn Euny is estimated to date from 1 BC and is unusual in that it has a circular side chamber which is said to have once had a corbelled roof. Something rather special in its day, one would suppose: a sort of de luxe version of the usual fougou. Fougous can be up to 60ft in length or even longer, so they must have had tremendous storage capacity if they were used for that purpose.

A fougou on the Trelowarren estate, known as Halligye Fougou, shown here, was recently examined and had some damage made good by the Historic Environmental Service of Cornwall County Council. The Iron Age fougou, one of the finest in Cornwall, was found to be the home of an important colony of horseshoe bats.

ST STEPHENS-BY-LAUNCESTON

95

Hidden Fossils

It is not uncommon to see fossils in church stonework. For instance, many of the pillars in Durham Cathedral, fashioned from the local Frosterley Marble, contain tiny fossil imprints of prehistoric corals, but in the church of St Stephen the Martyr, in the parish of St Stephens-by-Launceston there is something very different.

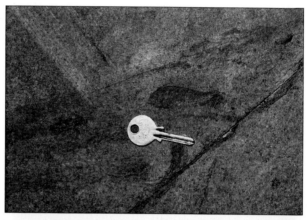

The floor of the entrance porch is comprised of very large slabs of slate and those slabs contain a secret seldom, if ever, seen, even by the church officers. The slabs are completely covered with a thick and very heavy coir mat, a safety measure for one thing, because slate gets very slippery when wet. And that mat has helped to preserve these unusual treasures.

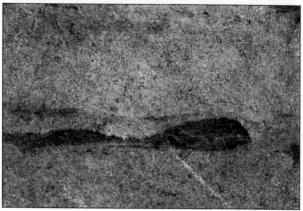

Imprinted in the slate are almost complete fossils of prehistoric fish and amphibians. They have been identified as: 1. Osteichthyes – a bony fish of the Devonian period. During that period Devon and Cornwall and the south of England were covered by a shallow sea. Devonian was in the Palaezoic era beginning some 395 million years ago. The first bony fish date from the Middle Devonian period. 2. Possibly Dipterus, a primitive lung fish with streamlined body and bony skeleton with a length of 15in. 3. Branchiosaurus, 2–3ft long. 4. Osteolepis, 9in long, Middle Devonian. One of the fossils appears to be a small newt-like creature.

Most of the slate used in this part of Cornwall comes from the gigantic Delabole Quarry, but the St Stephens fossils do not appear in Delabole slate, so no one knows from where the slate slabs in the porch originally came. It can be assumed that they were brought to the area many, many years ago because the church was built in Norman times.

96

STOKE CLIMSLAND

'The Temple'

Whiteford was at one time one of the finest parkland estates in Cornwall. Bought by John Call in 1763, it had everything going for it, and when it was inherited by his son, John Call, the new owner built a magnificent mansion and surrounded it with sumptuous gardens boasting fountains, statues and extravagant plantings. There was even a pleasure canal, complete with sluice gates, constructed in the valley. The house was equally grand, having granite staircases and furnished with every luxury of the period.

John Call, the son, was a military engineer who had very considerable business interests in the East India Company, through which he accumulated fabulous wealth. His house was unsurpassed in lavishness and was famed for its interior plasterwork created by foreign craftsmen. It also had a unique 'looking glass' room which was the sensation of the time.

Whiteford remained in the Call family until 1870 when the family fortunes plummeted and the estate was sold, passing through several owners until it was bought by the Duchy of Cornwall in 1879. The Duchy stripped the house and sold the contents, and in 1913 demolished the house, grounds and everything else in a dreadful act of vandalism which would today shock the world.

One of the buildings on the estate, the inspiration of John Call junior, was what has always been known as The Temple. It was both a type of folly and an 'eye-catcher', being built on the highest point on the estate and commanding extensive and beautiful views across parts of both Cornwall and Devon, which would impress visitors.

It also had a useful purpose, being designed as a summer retreat for grand and wild parties, dinners, suppers and possibly erotic entertainment. Miraculously, The Temple escaped the Duchy of Cornwall's destruction and it still stands proudly today, now leased by the Duchy to the Landmark Trust which has restored it and adapted it for letting as holiday accommodation.

The Temple is still most impressive, an iconic reminder of the splendours and excesses of the past. An indication of its original purpose is illustrated by the decorations on the front: stone tablets depicting the Muses of Greek mythology, the nine daughters of Zeus and Mnemosyne, who presided over the liberal arts. Clio was the muse of history; Enterpe of lyric poetry; Thalia of comedy and idyllic poetry; Melpomene of Tragedy; Terpsichore of music and dancing; Erato of amatory poetry; Calliope of epic poetry; Urania of astronomy and Polyhymnia of singing and harmony. Even today the building is a curious one, evocative of what was truly a liberal age, if you were wealthy enough to indulge in it.

STRATTON

The Stamford Hill Battle Memorial

97

Church pinnacles have been put to good use in Cornwall. One from St Mary's Church, Truro, is now a sundial, one from St Winnow Church is now a gatepost and one from Poughill church commemorates a battle.

The first decisive battle of the English Civil War took place over 360 years ago. The Battle of Stratton was fought on the escarpment now known as Stamford Hill, between the Parliamentarian troops led by the Earl of Stamford and the Royalist army of Cornwall led by Sir Ralph Hopton, and took place over ground between Bude and Stratton on 18 May 1643. The Royalist army, which included members of many of Cornwall's noblest families, trounced their opponents.

Such a historic site was naturally marked by a memorial and a curious one it is – a pinnacle from Poughill church surmounting a stone arch, surely the most unusual battle memorial in Britain. At one time there was also an old gun there but that had to be sacrificed in the Second World War, when all iron from railings to guns was urgently needed to make munitions.

Land over which the battle was fought is reputed to have yielded bumper crops of corn in the years following the peace, because, it is believed, the ground was well fertilised by the amount of human blood

shed on it. A macabre legend but one thought by many old Stratton folk to be true; in fact they could even name the farmers who harvested such fertile crops, with heads of corn so heavy with grain that they could barely remain upright.

In 1971 Bude & Stratton Old Cornwall Society placed a commemorative plaque on the memorial, and since 1977 the Sealed Knot Society has annually re-enacted the battle, a spectacle which attracts crowds of spectators.

98 ST TEATH AND POUNDSTOCK

'The King of Terrors' and 'The Rocket Man'

The inscriptions on old gravestones often bear testimony to how much our language and perceptions have changed over the years and sometimes they make unintentionally amusing reading to us today, although at the time they were probably regarded as remarkably graphic descriptions of those who ordered the wording of the unfortunate persons' demise. There are two outstanding examples: one in the churchyard at Poundstock, the other in the churchyard at St Teath.

The Poundstock one is rather enigmatic. It tells us that in 1785 'Francis Gubbin was in perfect Health at this Church on Sunday the 10th Day of July and was taken Captive by the King of Terrors July the 16th in the Blossom of his Age'. Just what was meant by the 'King of Terrors'? Was it intended to refer to the Devil? Did it refer to the scourge of an illness such as cholera or even the Black Death? We shall never know but somebody had very definite ideas about it at that time.

The other strange inscription is in St Teath churchyard where a gravestone informs us that 'George Harry of St Teath was suddenly launched into eternity 6th Feb. 1843 Aged 24', conjuring up pictures of space rockets – only in Cornwall could somebody have been inspired to compose that inscription!

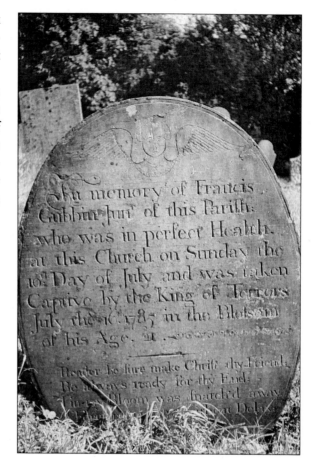

TEMPLE

99

The Knights Templars' Church

The tiny church of St Catherine on Bodmin Moor was once known as the Gretna Green of England and these days a less likely setting it would be hard to imagine. Temple church was originally built by the Knights Templars, one of three great orders of religious knights founded in the Holy Land at the time of the Crusades. The order was established in the year 1118 with the object of protecting pilgrims in Palestine and was confirmed by Pope Honorius II in 1128. The Templars set themselves up in England in 1185, with their headquarters at the Temple in Fleet Street, London.

The Templars built the church at Temple (which takes its name from them) as a resting place for pilgrims en route from Cornwall to the Holy Land and is virtually the last of the Templars' churches remaining outside London. The building we see today is not the original one. It is actually the third church on the site; the first was replaced by another on the same foundations, but that became derelict in the eighteenth century and was replaced by the present one in 1883, still exactly on the original foundations. It was designed by Cornish architect Sylvanus Trevail, famous throughout Cornwall as the designer of many nineteenth-century churches and chapels in the county.

The little church we see today is very basic but it has one crowning glory – the stained-glass window above the altar at the east end of the church, which is dominated by the red cross symbol of the Crusaders. The colours are bright and clear and the window is really very lovely.

Why that reputation as the Gretna Green of England? Because the Knights Templars were not subject to Bishopric visits – vicars had the right to marry people without licence or banns. So Temple church was popular with couples wanting to elope, perhaps against the wishes of their families. It was certainly not looked upon very favourably by the good Cornish people, who were totally disapproving. Equally unpopular was the edict that suicides could be buried in consecrated ground at Temple. All that no longer applies so would-be brides and bridegrooms need not rush off to Cornwall.

The churchyard has one grave which always attracts particular attention. With the passage of time the granite cross on a rough hewn boulder from Bodmin Moor which stands above the grave has become covered with a rough grey-green lichen which gives it an unearthly appearance. There is a sad story about the one who lies beneath it.

On 13 January 1901 the Revd Charles Ernest Lambert, rector of Warleggan and former vicar of Temple, died on the moor while walking back to Warleggan after officiating at evensong at Temple. His body was not discovered until three days later and during that time his faithful and much loved Irish terrier remained at its master's side, whimpering from time to time in a vain attempt to summon help.

It is well worth making a short detour off the nearby and very busy A30 road to visit Temple church.

TINTAGEL

A Poignant Memorial

In the graveyard of St Materiana's Church at Tintagel is an unusual and poignant grave marker. The churchyard is in a very windswept location and even the normal gravestones are supported at the backs by stone buttresses to ensure that they stay upright.

Among these more conventional stones is a unique form of commemoration. It is a ship's lifebelt fixed to a plain wooden cross; on the lifebelt are painted the words 'Catanese Domenico "Iota" 1893 Napoli'. It marks the grave of a young boy who perished at sea off the treacherous cliffs over 100 years ago. On the afternoon of 21 December 1893 the three-masted iron barque *Iota* of Naples was on passage from Cardiff to Trinidad when it was swept on to the deadly Lye rock below Willapark. The crew abandoned ship and jumped on to the rocks, but three of them failed to reach safety, including the young cabin boy Catanese Domenico, who was carried away by the mountainous seas. His body was washed up a few days later and buried in Tintagel churchyard.

A funeral service was conducted by Anglican rite but the officiating clergyman said the Lord's Prayer in Latin over the simple grave, the only common language he could share with the boy to link him with his Roman Catholic upbringing.

To this day the lifebelt and cross are kept in immaculate condition and young Catanese Domenico is never forgotten by the good folk of this town.

TINTAGEL

101

Rocky Valley Carvings

Rocky Valley in the Bossiney area of Tintagel is a romantic but slightly awe-inspiring location. At one time it supported industry, and the ruins of both a fulling mill and a corn mill are still there. But the most remarkable and mysterious thing about Rocky Valley is some strange carving in the hard rock.

Britain's late Neolithic and early Bronze Age people carved curious symbols on outcrop rock faces. They obviously all had some importance or significance, but what? On a rock face in Rocky Valley are two labyrinth-style designs dating back, it is thought, from 1800 to 1400 BC,

the early Bronze Age. Their true purpose is unknown although experts claim there is indisputable evidence that they were sacred or religious symbols.

In the north of England and parts of Scotland there are similar examples of this form of primitive art, and they have been found in connection with burial sites, on standing stones and cist covers.

Although many eminent archaeologists have examined and discussed the carvings, none have hazarded a firm opinion on the cultural or religious significance of the carvings. Could it have been that the carvings were intended to be trance-inducing? To stare at them for any length of time has a mildly hypnotic effect.

There is one curious phenomenon with the Rocky Valley carvings: when photographed they always appear to have dappling on them; it is not caused by the shadow of overhanging leaves or lichen on the stone.

These are the only known examples in Cornwall, so a real curiosity not to be missed if one is prepared to walk the narrow, uneven path above the river to reach them. The carvings are now preserved by English Heritage and the rough footpath above the 'canyon' is a public right of way.

TORPOINT

The Topiary Arbour

102

Topiary is becoming an increasingly popular aspect of gardening. It is a highly skilled art and very time consuming because constant trimming is necessary to keep the weird and wonderful designs created in pristine condition.

It would be hard to find a larger or more ambitious topiary feature than the arbour in the grounds of Antony House, a National Trust property. This massive cone-shaped tree has an arched entrance and one can go inside and sit on the seat there, perfectly protected from the elements. A gardener must need to stand on a 'cherry picker' platform to be able to clip the top of the cone. It is kept in immaculate condition with never a twig or leaf growing out to spoil the line. It is, after all, a living thing, so is constantly growing and needing attention. It is a gardening feat extraordinaire.

103

TRURO

The Cathedral Beam

So inconspicuous it is rarely noticed, there is an odd small piece of blue glass in the middle of the handsome stained-glass window above the High Altar in Truro Cathedral which has quite a curious story attached to it.

In the dark days of the Second World War a young schoolboy was taking potshots at the flagpole on the nearby old Cathedral Grammar School building; he was using a First World War rifle and firing from his bedroom window at his home in Bridge Street. But his aim was disastrous and instead he shot through the window of the cathedral. As an urgent temporary measure in 1945 a local builder replaced the damaged glass with an ordinary piece of blue glass, the only thing available at the time.

That piece of glass is still there because the builder later declined to work at 200ft above the ground again and no one else was prepared to rise to those heights either. But it provides an almost magical sight. If the sun is shining between 6.45 and 7 a.m. on 1 September the sun exactly strikes the piece of glass and sends a magical purplish-blue beam the whole length of the nave. The beam then travels from pillar to pillar, finally resting on the floor at the west end of the cathedral. Cathedral staff say that if there is dust in the air the beam is intensified. This strange phenomenon is also witnessed at other times as a spot of colour around the chancel steps. It is worth watching for if visiting the cathedral on a sunny day.

104

TRURO

An Expensive Convenience

The rapidly rising cost of property in Cornwall was highlighted not long ago when a tiny little building, a former men's public convenience, in the centre of Truro was declared redundant and put up for sale. The estate agents reported so much interest in purchasing it that talk of five-figure sums was being bandied about. When the sale finally took place the building was bought by the Devon and Cornwall Constabulary for £5,000. A blue lamp was put on its roof and it was presumably to be used as an emergency telephone station. However, the police evidently found that it did not meet their requirements after all and they sold it on to Social Services – for £8,000. At the time of writing this is not yet in use, so speculation remains about its future purpose.

Cornwall has lots of odd little buildings like that and when put on the market they turn out to be gold mines for their owners. Pigs' houses, redundant public conveniences, wagon sheds, dog kennels, they are all in demand and prove to be good investments, even if they were originally only built by the farmer and his labourer to house the Christmas 'porker'.

TRURO

The Pinnacle Sundial

105

Sundials are commonplace in Cornish churches and churchyards but at Truro there is one that is unique. In the grounds of Diocesan House, the administrative centre for Truro Cathedral, is a sundial, which was originally the top of the spire of the old St Mary's Church. It was incorporated into the cathedral when that building was erected in the late nineteenth century.

Another difference about it is that the gnomon is in the shape of a cross but it is unfortunately not accurately aligned, so not advisable to set one's watch by it. Carved around the base of the sundial is a gentle and thought-provoking inscription which reads:

> High above busy Truro town,
> Of Mary's church this topmost crown
> Has borne through a century's space
> The holy word of Christ's dear grace.
> Now in Escop's garden ground
> As sunlit hours go circling round,
> This shadowed cross shall mark and bless
> My days of leisured quietness.

TRURO

Statues not Pinnacles

106

St Paul's Church, Truro, beside one of the main arteries into the city, is a fine building, but not everyone travelling up and down the busy main road notices a most unusual feature about it. The central tower is crowned not with the usual pinnacles but with statues of three eminent Cornishmen of days long past.

The statues are of Bishop Trelawny, Richard Grenville and Sir John Eliot, the fourth pinnacle place being a turret. Sir Jonathan Trelawny was one of the famous seven bishops who according to Arthur Mee, 'risked their lives for conscience sake and sounded the death knell of the Stuart dynasty'. In 1688 Trelawny stood trial as one of those seven bishops who faced death rather than yield to the Declaration by which James II wanted to restore Roman Catholicism to England. At his trial Trelawny was acquitted and became a Cornish hero, and the subject of what is now known as the 'Cornish national anthem', written by the Revd R.S. Hawker. Trelawny died in 1720.

Richard Grenville, born in 1541, was a cousin of Sir Walter Raleigh and a friend of Sir Francis Drake. He was famed for his sea battles

against the Spaniards and he died a prisoner of the Spanish. He will always be remembered as one of England's greatest sailors and for his tremendous courage.

Sir John Eliot was regarded as one of our greatest Parliamentarians and was deeply anguished at the execution of Sir Walter Raleigh. He was imprisoned and released by subsequent kings and finally died while imprisoned in the Tower of London by King Charles I. He was buried in the precincts of the Tower because the King refused to allow his body to be taken home to Cornwall for burial.

TRURO
Work it Out!

On a wall in the vestibule of an imposing building in the centre of Truro, formerly the Market Hall and now the Hall for Cornwall, is an inscribed tablet dating from 1615 which when examined for the first time looks to be gibberish, but further inspection and a little thought reveal it to be not so. The carved stone tablet was originally on the wall of the market house and town hall built in 1615, the market hall being open-sided. When this market hall was demolished in the early nineteenth century the tablet was removed first to the new market hall in Boscawen Street and then in the mid-nineteenth century to its successor, the building which still graces the main street in the city.

A large section of the tablet is taken up with what appears to be a shield depicting a sailing ship and some incomprehensible lettering by the side of the shield. This is where de-coding comes in. The message at the base of the tablet was intended to encourage honesty among the market traders and the letters above refer to the person who was instrumental in having a market hall erected. The horizontal lettering, 'IEN', does not appear to mean anything but then it is remembered that 'I' was the old way of writing the letter 'J'. On reading down the lettering becomes clear: 'Jenken, Daniel. Mayor'.

The Daniel family of Kenwyn were important merchants in Truro in the seventeenth century. Of the seven sons of Alexander and Agnes Daniel, Richard was sent in 1579 to work for a merchant in London. He was apprenticed to a local merchant and later became a merchant and draper in Truro. In 1614 Jenken became Mayor of Truro and during that year the open-sided market house and town hall were built, so his name was inscribed on the tablet. The depiction of the fully rigged sailing ship in the shield on the tablet may have been an allusion to the fact that Richard Daniel, younger brother of David, had married a wealthy widow in the Low Countries and prospered, later lending considerable sums of money to David to help the latter develop his own business.

The inscription at the bottom of the tablet, reading the letter 'U' for 'V' and despite no punctuation, says 'Who seeks to find eternal treasure must use no guile in weight or measure'. In other words, don't cheat the customers in any way!

Few people notice the tablet as they hurry in and out of the busy building, but it is a bit of old Truro not to be missed.

108 TYWARDREATH

England's Last Private Chapel

Cornwall can claim several records of one kind and another, but there is a little-known one of which the county can boast – the last private chapel to be built in England was erected here in the early nineteenth century.

In times gone by wealthy landowners and members of the aristocracy would construct their own places of worship on their estates and little Tregaminion Chapel of Ease is no exception. It is on the Rashleigh estate, near the entrance to Menabilly House, famous as the one-time home of novelist Daphne du Maurier.

The chapel was built by William Rashleigh in 1913 on a site he himself selected and the foundation stone was laid by his wife Mrs Rachel Rashleigh. Sadly, Rachel died only a few months after work on the chapel commenced but her husband pressed on with the project, which was now to become a memorial to his wife. However, two years after Rachel's death William married his second wife, Caroline, in the same year that Tregaminion Chapel of Ease was opened for worship. Every Sunday the Rashleigh family, their servants, estate workers and some of their tenants attended service in the chapel.

In 1957 the chapel was taken over by the Church Commissioners and in the early 1980s extensive repairs were carried out on the building, which had deteriorated with age.

The most recent occasion of note in the chapel was the memorial service for the late Daphne du Maurier, whose home at Menabilly featured in one of her novels. She used to attend service in the chapel. Services are held regularly in the chapel with the vicar of Tywardreath officiating at them. The chapel has many tributes to the Rashleigh family within it, the family coat of arms being prominently depicted in the windows.

WANSON MOUTH, NEAR BUDE

'Tortoise' Stones

Wanson Mouth is not the easiest of beaches to reach but it does contain something very unusual in the form of what are known locally as 'tortoise' stones. They are a natural curiosity not seen elsewhere in Cornwall and their nickname is very apt. Actually they are concretions, the dictionary definition being 'an aggregation of particles into a more or less regular ball'. We are told by those who profess to know that when the earth was cooling aeons ago bubbles were being formed on the surface and these bubbles became filled with some volcanic material. As they cooled they and the material within them hardened and formed the tortoise stones.

Whatever the explanations, these concretions are very strange. For one thing they are deposited in straight lines down the beach towards the sea, almost like miniature groynes, and they are all embedded standing up on their edges. They get washed out with the tides and can be picked up on the beach. They are extremely heavy and the best-shaped ones, being rounded on the top but flat on the bottom, resemble the carapace of a tortoise.

What is not easy to explain is why they all have a line around the middle, as though they are two halves stuck together, and those split open by the action of the sea and lying in halves on the beach show a clean and clear division as if split with a chisel, like a slate. As far as is known, the tortoise stones at Wanson Mouth are not like any other concretions elsewhere.

110

WENDRON AND WERRINGTON

Black Slaves' Graves

They came to these shores in their thousands, they were used and valued for the work they could do but when they died they did so in obscurity and no one wanted to remember them. They were black slaves, brought from Africa and elsewhere in the eighteenth century and particularly exploited by the wealthier classes, for whom they often worked.

There are no more than a dozen headstones erected over the graves of slaves in the whole of the British Isles, and Cornwall is fortunate in having two of these rare stones. The older of these two is fixed against the north wall of the church in Werrington churchyard, having originally stood in the graveyard of the old church in Werrington Park until demolished by Sir William Morice, who also had the graveyard levelled.

Philip Scipio was brought to England by Philip, Duke of Wharton, who had acquired him in St Helena. Wharton's sister was Lady Lucy Morice, wife of Sir William of Werrington Park. The Duke, accompanied by his slave, was visiting the Morices when he had to flee the country. He was a notorious philanderer, and when his misdeeds caught up with him he hastily departed for Spain, leaving his slave behind.

Lady Lucy took the young boy on as her personal servant, and when he died at the age of 18 years, unable to survive the English weather she had a stone bearing a glowing epitaph raised above his grave in the old churchyard. The stone was not discovered until the late nineteenth century, when it was being used as a paving stone on a farm in the parish. It was brought to the church and fixed to the exterior of the north wall near a Morice grave.

The other stone, in Wendron 'new' churchyard opposite the church, tells a different story and is unique in that master and slave are buried together in the same grave.

Everisto Muchovela, a native of Mozambique, was conveyed by slave ship to Rio de Janeiro at the age of 7 and there purchased by Mr Thomas Johns, a mining engineer of Porkellis, Cornwall. Evaristo remained in his service for twenty-two years. When Mr Johns died in 1861 he left Evaristo a legacy and requested that they be buried in the same grave.

Evaristo died in 1868 at the age of 38 and the joint tombstone reads:

> Here lie the master and the slave
> Side by side within one grave.
> Distinction's lost and caste is o'er.
> The slave is now a slave no more.

Sacred to the
Memory of
THOMAS JOHNS.
of Porkellis.
who departed this life.
January 28th 1861.
AGED 61 YEARS.

God my Redeemer, lives,
And ever from the skies
Looks down and watches all my dust,
Till he shall bid it rise.

EVARISTO MUCHOVELA
born in Mosambique. South Africa.
died at Redruth Feb.ry 19th 1868.
AGED 38 YEARS.

Here lie the master and the slave
side by side within one grave.
distinction's lost and caste is oer.
the slave is now a slave no more.

111 WERRINGTON

The Civil War Tree

There was heavy fighting and some serious battles fought in Werrington, near Launceston, in the Civil War; several cannon balls have been found and a musket ball was found embedded in the cob wall of an old cottage. But there is one survivor of the conflict which is still alive – although battered it is still standing.

Not far from the boundary of Werrington Cricket Club's ground is a very ancient tree which, if it could talk, could tell some stirring tales of those bloodthirsty times. This very fine ancient oak tree, old even at the time of the battles, was blasted by cannon fire to such an extent that it became completely hollow, so much so that children can today climb up inside it. But it is remarkable in that it is still thriving and produces leaves every year. Up until a few years ago it even bore acorns. It is a living link with life as it was almost five centuries ago.

The tree is on private land but is accessible by walking through a field gate and across a field, but permission must be sought before visiting it.

Oak trees tend to get hollow as they grow very old, but this one was affected in its comparative youth because of the battering it had as warfare raged around it. It is certainly the oldest living thing in Werrington.

WERRINGTON

Cullacott Wall Paintings

Cullacott has been described as the most important medieval house in Cornwall and in the late 1990s it underwent a £400,000 restoration which revealed some exciting and unique features.

In 1579 Walter Blyghte became the tenant at Cullacott and he made some sweeping changes to the old house. He was obviously a gentleman who fancied his position in life and he had his name and the date carved on the granite lintel of the parlour window, and even installed a heated garderobe (a medieval loo).

Mr Blyghte had delusions of grandeur and one of the 'must have' things he craved was tapestries on the walls of the hall. Every gentleman's dwelling had tapestries, but such refinements cost money even in those days and Mr Blyghte was perhaps not quite as well endowed with cash as some affluent landowners. But he was an ingenious man and was not going to be outshone by wealthier contemporaries. So he would fool them into thinking that he had tapestries too – if they did not look too closely.

Mr Blyghte had designs painted on his walls. Above the paintings are nails driven into the wall and painted cords to imitate a tapestry hanging on the wall, rather than just a painting. Since there was no electric light in those days it is unlikely that anyone noticed the deception. At least Mr Blyghte wins top marks for ingenuity!

WERRINGTON

113

Twin Towers

When the cantankerous and unpredictable Sir William Morice, the third and last baronet, was resident at Werrington Park, near Launceston, in the mid-eighteenth century, he decided he wanted a bowling green on his property. The site he chose for it was very inappropriately just where the parish church, St Martin of Tours's, then stood, quite near to his mansion.

It was a calamitous decision as far as the parishioners were concerned, but Sir William went ahead and had the church demolished; all the gravestones were dug up and either smashed or used as paving stones. Just two survived and are in the present churchyard. This vandalism naturally infuriated the parishioners who promptly put a curse on the Morice family; strangely, this proved most effective.

In the meantime, Sir William had to provide another church, which he did, under an Act granted in 1740, outside the boundaries of Werrington Park, where it stands today. Sir William mainly designed the new church himself and gave it one very distinctive feature. He had the tower flanked by two replicas of it. They are quite solid and are a conspicuous feature which make the church the only one in Cornwall with three towers.

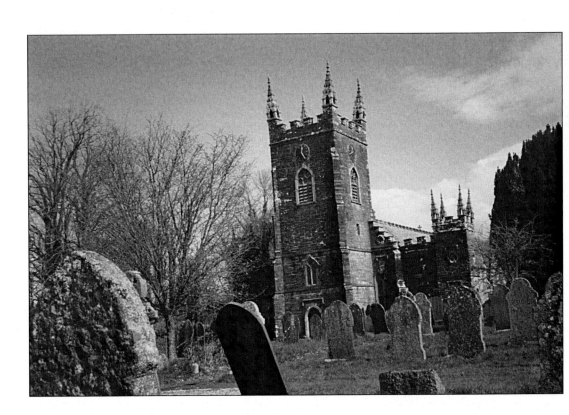

But William Morice did not have a lot of time to enjoy either his bowling green or his new church. He died without issue in 1749 and it seems the parishioners' curse had started to work. The Morice family fortunes dwindled so alarmingly that within thirty years all the vast Morice estates had passed to strangers and today no traces of the Morice family are visible within the church. The only tangible reminder is a small piece of an ornate marble tomb of the first baronet (who died in 1688), and which was in the original church.

When the present church was extended in Victorian times and a new vestry built, the fragment of the tomb, in the shape of a heart, was cemented into the wall of the inner vestry; as that small room is kept locked the tablet is unseen by the general public. Some years ago there was a suggestion to remove the tablet and place it on a wall in the church but it was found to be too thin; it was feared that it would crumble if any attempt was made to move it. So the curse of the Morice family appears to be still in existence, and they are no longer revered or indeed feared as they once were.

WERRINGTON   **114**

The Sugar Loaves

Follies were rich men's obsessions in the eighteenth century. If you had a country estate you had to have at least one folly on it, and the aim was always to erect something more unusual or outrageous than your contemporaries.

Such was the motive which inspired the eccentric second Sir William Morice of Werrington Park when he conceived the idea of the Sugar Loaves. Not that it was his intention that they should be called that. In keeping with the times and interest in classical sculptures, it is believed the Sugar Loaves was designed as a personalised copy of the celebrated tomb at Albano, Italy, some 12 miles south of Rome, of the Horatii and the Curiatii – brothers who as duellists, recklessly perhaps, decided the quarrel between these impious neighbours must be settled with their lives. They are buried near the highway. Sir William Morice may have seen the monument while on a Grand Tour and decided that was what he would have in his park.

In addition to the Werrington Sugar Loaves, Sir William had other follies built in the grounds, but this is the only one that still survives. It is sited on rising ground with a magnificent view across the valley of the River Attery to Sir William's house and consists of two massive conical structures on a rectangular stone platform containing embrasures and seats so that Sir William and his guests could sit and gaze across at the mansion of which he was so proud.

It was in later years, long after Sir William's demise, that the monument was dubbed the Sugar Loaves because the pinnacles resembled the cones of sugar which were produced in olden times.

A decade ago, when there was an extensive felling of trees in Smallacombe Copse, the Sugar Loaves was visible from the public road, but since then trees and vegetation have grown up around it and it is once again hidden from view.

The folly is on private land and there is no public access to it. Sir William Morice constructed an entrance into Werrington Park from Dutson hamlet, passing through Smallacombe Copse and close to the Sugar Loaves, but it is now only a rough grass track, barely discernible.

WIDEMOUTH BAY

The Salt House

115

Widemouth Bay is now a very popular residential area as well as being famed for its sands and surf. In the Domesday Book of 1086 no fewer than ten salthouses were listed in the manor of Stratton, and The Salt House was one of them.

Salt panning took place in the area in Roman times; that has been confirmed by the discovery of pottery dating from that era which was found in the salt-panning area of Widemouth Bay in 1964. Salt panning continued into the Middle Ages and the Widemouth Bay Salt House at one time stood on the coastal highway until erosion washed it away. N.J.G. Pounds, who mapped the Cornish Fish Cellars in 1944, described the building as being of stone 'plastered and colour washed' and with rag slate roof. It was one of the ten listed by him from the Domesday Survey. Single fish cellars, as this one, were associated with the seine net fishing industry and were used for salting pilchards.

The Widemouth building has had many extensions over the years, but the original old building still stands and is Grade II listed. It was severely damaged by fire a few years ago but has since been restored.

116

ST WINNOW

Pinnacle Gatepost

Granite gateposts are common enough in Cornwall, but a real curiosity is a pinnacle from a church tower serving that purpose.

'Waste not, want not' was obviously the philosophy of the parishoners of St Winnow in days long past. The Civil War had a disastrous effect on some of Cornwall's church towers and St Winnow parish came through it pretty badly. The church was in the thick of the fighting and

as the battle raged around it the tower fell in ruins. The pinnacles from this and some of the stone from little St Nectan's Chapel lying around the churchyard were put to good use. One of the pinnacles is used as a gatepost at the entrance to the churchyard and some of the stones serve as steps, the rest of the masonry being used for any purpose for which a big stone would come in handy.

The remains of the church were roofed and today the building presents a rather strange appearance with its truncated tower, but at least its pinnacle proved useful.

ZENNOR

The Mermaid

117

The Mermaid of Zennor is an old tale with which almost every Cornishman and woman is familiar from their earliest days. It is of such long standing that nearly as far back as medieval times some craftsman carved a bench end for Zennor church depicting the mermaid.

The story goes that a beautiful young woman wearing a garment that swept the ground sat regularly at the back of the church. She was

entranced by the singing of a local lad, Matthew Trewhella, who was one of the choristers in the church. One evening she lured him with the charms of her own singing to a little stream which ran through the village on its way to the sea. The woman was a mermaid, who led Matthew down the stream to Mermaid's Cove; together they entered the sea, never to be seen again.

However, the legend says that they return to the cove and on summer nights when the moon is high and the air still, they can be heard singing together above the sound of the splash of the waves.

Modern folk singers have adopted the romantic legend and have written songs around it, one singer even taking as her stage name the Mermaid of Zennor.

Occasionally some people still claim that they have heard the couple performing their duet, and a few years ago someone tried to record it on tape but was unsuccessful, despite claiming to have the most modern foolproof equipment. Matthew and his mermaid are obviously publicity shy!

Evidently the ancient carver who depicted the mermaid believed in the story. Now the church houses the Mermaid's Chair, made partly of two ancient bench ends which form the sides of the little seat. The carving on the bench ends is of a mermaid examining herself in the mirror she holds in one hand, while in the other she holds a comb with which she grooms her long tresses.

The church, dedicated to St Senara, underwent a complete restoration in the late nineteenth century and it is thought that the bench ends were made into a chair at that time. It is believed the carvings go back to the sixteenth century when those skilled and clever craftsmen depicted life as they knew it then and included the legends that everybody knew and understood – and, most importantly, believed.

118 ZENNOR

Last person to speak Cornish

People coming to Cornwall for the first time may well read or hear somewhere about Dolly Pentreath, who was the last woman to speak Cornish as her native tongue. That is correct in a sense, but Dolly was not the last person to speak only Cornish and nothing else.

To honour the Memory of
JOHN DAVEY, of Boswednack
in this Parish (b.St.Just:1812:d.Boswednack,1891)
who was the last to possess any considerable
Traditional Knowledge of the Cornish Language,
& that of his Father & instructor JOHN DAVEY
of St.Just (b.Boswednack,1770:d.St.Just,1844)
well known as a Mathematician & Schoolmaster,
both of whom lie buried near this Stone was
set up by the St.Ives Old Cornwall Society
1930.
Gerióu Ganov Den yu kepar ha Dowrow down
ha Fenten Skyans avel Gover ov resek a'n prav

On the wall in the entrance porch of Zennor church is a memorial tablet to John Davey, who really was the last person to speak Cornish as his native tongue and who died in 1891, long after Dolly, who died in 1777. Where Mr Davey scores over his more famous rival is that although Dolly spoke Cornish as her native tongue, she also spoke English, whereas John Davey could not speak any language other than Cornish. He is known and honoured for this by all Cornish people but little is known of him and he is given no publicity outside his native county.

On the other hand, Dolly is known almost worldwide and had an ornate memorial erected to her memory, which, because of the story behind it, has helped to boost and publicise her false claim.

Prince Louis Lucien Bonaparte was interested in Dolly's ability to speak Cornish and in 1860 had an elaborate memorial constructed in St Paul's churchyard to honour her. It says it was built 'in union with the Revd John Gabbett, vicar of St Paul'. By contrast John Davey's tablet is very plain and unpretentious.

POSTSCRIPT

What is it?

All good 'whodunnits' end with a mystery on which the reader can put their own interpretation if they so wish. This book does not fall into that category but ends with a Cornish mystery of long ago for which some-one, somewhere, might have an authentic explanation.

For a number of years Steve Hartgroves, senior archaeologist of the Historic Environment Service of Cornwall County Council has been engaged on a project which entails photographing and mapping all historical features of Cornwall from the air with particular emphasis on prehistoric features such as fortifications, etc., visible only from the air and completely unseen at ground level. This ambitious project has revealed a wealth of information and a priceless record of prehistoric man's activities in the county. Most of the ramparts, ditches, settlement sites and so on have been identified and logged, but one remains a total mystery.

In a field at Trecrogo, South Petherwin, near Launceston, there is visible only from the air a vast pattern of four concentric rings with a 'bullseye' in the middle, resembling an immense archery target. The rings are perfect circles, the outer circle having a diameter of about 260ft, the inner one 55ft. The feature is within an area of concentrated prehistoric activity, being sited near two Bronze Age barrows, a possible prehistoric field system and round.

The experts at the Historic Environment Service have no idea what its purpose could have been, pointing out that barrows and henges do not look like this.

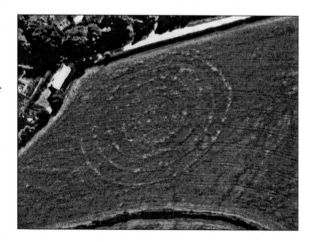

The regularity of the circles has suggested perhaps a Second World War military feature, possibly some kind of radar display, but it does not show on RAF aerial photographs from 1946 and local residents living in the area during the war have no knowledge of such an installation in their midst. As the circles are in a field adjacent to a public road any wartime installation would have been clearly visible to everyone passing it. So what is it? It is a real Cornish curiosity in more ways than one and a fitting item to conclude this book about dear, odd Cornwall, full of mysteries!

BIBLIOGRAPHY AND SOURCES

Books
Acton, Bob, *A View from Trencrom*, Landfall Publications, 1992
Carne, Tony, *Cornwall's Forgotten Corner*, Lodenak Press, 1985
Dunn, Mike, *The Looe Island Story*, Polperro Heritage
Headley, Gwyn and Meullnkamp, Wm, *Follies*, Jonathan Cape, 1986
Harris, K., Hevva – *Cornish Fishing in the Days of Sail*, Dyllanson, Truran, 1983
Mais, S.P.B., *The Cornish Riviera*, Great Western Railway Company, 1928
Mee, Arthur, *The King's England – Cornwall*, Hodder & Stoughton, 1949
Sagar, Michael and Smith, Stuart B., *Serpentine*, Truran, 2005
Woodhouse, Harry, *Cornish Bagpipes*, Dyllanson, Truran (nd)

Useful Publications and Sources
Church magazine of St Cleer, Pensilva and St Ive Parishes
Cornwall Historic Churches Trust
Old Cornwall, journal of the Federation of Old Cornwall Societies
Historic Environment Service, Cornwall County Council
The Landmark Trust
The National Trust
Penzance Tourist information Office – Penwith District Council
Walks Around Camelford, North Cornwall District Council

Church Leaflets
Gunwalloe
Minster
Morvah
Kilkhampton
St Mawgan in Meneage